DELICIOUSLY SIMPLE

Jane Lovett

DELICIOUSLY SIMPLE

Fast, fuss-free recipes
for any occasion

Photography by Tony Briscoe

For Sal, with my love and thanks.

xx

Also by Jane Lovett:

Make it Easy

The Get-Ahead Cook

Just One Pan

Contents

Introduction

Quick cooking is the essence of *Deliciously Simple*, with emphasis on 'cooking'. There's a fine line between making a speedy recipe requiring only limited cooking and minimum effort, and producing one through unmitigated cheating, often involving no actual cooking whatsoever. And so, while speed is the thread running through the recipes, cooking also remains firmly at the heart of them.

As an instinctive feeder, I always strive to create simple, accessible and appealing food that people really want to eat, and I hope through this book you will see that the added emphasis on speed doesn't have to mean uninventive or uninspiring. *Deliciously Simple* is bursting with tasty recipes requiring minimum effort. They are delicious and beautifully presented, achievable for cooks of all abilities, and aren't demanding, even for a novice cook.

These recipes are straightforward yet imaginative. They're swift to make, though never speedy for speed's sake. They sometimes include a few shortcuts, plus, of course, the odd cheat along the way for added convenience. I've left out laborious techniques, such as blind-baking a pastry case, and anything that involves multiple methods.

Using the Book

My hope is that from within these pages you'll be able to produce delicious food as quickly as possible for most occasions; from picnics to supper parties, snacking to casual eating at home, right through to entertaining – be it drinks and canapés, dinner parties or larger feasts. Most recipes have instructions for advance preparation, which should help greatly and be invaluable towards these ends, too.

One reviewer kindly described my last book, *Just One Pan*, as 'the sort of cook book you'll use all the time', and that's exactly what I set out to offer with this book as well. I'm confident you'll be able to dip in and out and produce wonderful recipes for any moment. Above all, I really hope you will enjoy planning menus, cooking the recipes, and those gatherings, too, of course!

The Quick Cook's Handy Kitchen 'Helpers'

When in a hurry, or to speed up a recipe, using a mixture of fresh ingredients and precooked food is perfectly acceptable in my view. Nevertheless, I would advise buying the best quality you can afford, produced by reputable brands. In most cases, these products have the added advantage of a long shelf life, so, as well as speed, they offer endless other store cupboard recipe opportunities. It's also comforting to have up one's sleeve the ability to pull something tasty out of the hat at short notice. That said, you'll find the majority of these recipes don't require precooked ingredients.

It's worth remembering that smaller cuts of meat cook far more quickly than whole joints – think chicken breasts, legs, thighs and tenders (inner breast fillets); duck breasts; pork tenderloin; lamb rump, chops and neck fillet; beef steaks. Fish fillets are quicker to cook (around 5 minutes) than whole fish, and prawns only take a minute or two. All of these are ideal for speedy cooking.

You've probably discovered all sorts of other shortcuts, tricks and hacks, which I have yet to find. Overleaf I've included some that I use, and generally have on standby for when speed is of the essence.

Perishable Shortcut Foods

- Frozen chopped onions (a relatively new revelation for me). Available from most supermarkets, they are a gift for quick cooking.

- Ready-made (chilled or frozen) shortcrust, sweet shortcrust, puff and filo pastries – these are big time-savers, especially puff and filo pastries, as they are time-consuming and require skill to make. Buy blocks, or even speedier, ready-rolled sheets.

- Fresh stock, which can then be frozen, if necessary.

- Fresh pesto – I make my own (see page 17).

- Fresh mayonnaise – I make my own (see page 17).

- Spring onions – quick to prepare and cook, and can sometimes be substituted for onions, which take longer to cook.

- Fresh egg or rice noodles, which can then be frozen, if necessary.

Ambient Shortcuts (some of these need storing in the fridge once opened)

- Stock pots (quicker than dissolving stock cubes), stock cubes, pouches of stock.

- Balsamic syrup.

- Prepared herbs, ginger, wasabi and garlic in squeezy tubes.

- Puréed ginger and puréed lemon grass in jars.

- Pouches of cooked rice and other grains (sometimes mixed), plain, or seasoned or spiced with different flavours.

- Pouches of cooked beans and pulses, sometimes with added flavourings.

- Tinned pulses and beans.

- Roasted red peppers in jars.

- Roasted artichoke hearts, in jars or tins.

- 'Straight-to-wok' noodles (or similar).

- Dried noodles.

- Ready-cooked pastry cases; large or individual.

Cook's Notes

1. All eggs used in the recipes are large and free-range.

2. All butter used in the recipes is lightly salted.

3. Salt refers to table salt throughout, unless sea salt flakes are specified in the recipe.

4. Full-fat ingredients are used throughout the book, but you can substitute, depending on personal preference. However, bear in mind that this might affect the end result and that some reduced fat dairy products separate when heated.

5. Herbs are all fresh unless stated as dried. Fresh or dried bay leaves can be used in relevant recipes.

6. If you are vegetarian, please ensure that the cheese you use is suitable for vegetarians. Vegetarian options for alternative cheeses are mentioned in some recipes, but always check the packaging to be certain that the cheese is suitable.

7. All recipes assume that raw ingredients are at room temperature before going into the oven.

8. Ovens should be preheated to the specified temperatures. I used a non-fan (conventional) electric oven for all the recipes. Fan (and gas) oven temperatures are also given, but do consult your oven manual if using a fan oven (though generally the temperature is 20°C lower than the conventional one given, as shown in the recipes).

9. Spoon measures are level unless stated otherwise. Use a set of measuring spoons for accurate measuring. A teaspoon is 5ml, a tablespoon is 15ml.

General Notes

1. Always read through a recipe fully before going shopping for it and before getting started.

2. Seasoning is imperative to good-tasting food. Season as you go along rather than as an afterthought, and season each component or step of a recipe, as directed.

3. Piping hot food has little or no taste or flavour, so it's always advisable to allow a finished hot dish to cool down for a few minutes before serving. If steam is in evidence when the dish is cut or spooned into, this is a good indicator that the food is too hot to eat.

4. Recipes and ingredients attributed to different countries and cultures are not authentic, simply my interpretation of them, inspired by ingredients and occasionally food I've enjoyed in those countries.

5. Some recipes have suggested substitutes, although I would urge you to put your stamp on them, according to your tastes, the season and what you have to hand.

6. Two ready-made products which I feel aren't ideal replacements for the real thing are mayonnaise and pesto sauce. Mayonnaise is used throughout the book and obviously buying it fresh or ready-made from a jar is the quickest option. If taking this route, I would recommend choosing the best quality as well as a brand without a distinct flavour, which in turn permeates throughout the dish. (For me, a universally popular, well-known brand of mayo falls into the distinct flavour category. Very good as a product on its own, but in my view, because of its distinct flavour, it's best not incorporated into a recipe.) The same goes for pesto sauce from a jar, which I feel never quite lives up to expectations either, lacking both the flavour and colour of fresh basil and the zing of the traditional sauce.

7. However, help is at hand with these very quick methods for making home-made mayonnaise and pesto. They literally take minutes to make (almost as quick as unscrewing the lid of a jar!) and I think are well worth it for the superior taste they will bring to the recipes.

Super-speedy Stick Blender Mayonnaise

Put 2 egg yolks (at room temperature), a generous ½ tablespoon of English mustard, ½ tablespoon of fresh lemon juice (or white wine vinegar) and ½ teaspoon of salt into the beaker of a stick blender (or a tall, narrow jug or tall jam jar – I make and store mine in a tall, narrow, round airtight container) and top with 150ml of vegetable oil and 50ml of olive oil.

Stand the blender firmly on the bottom of the beaker/container, tilt it slightly and whizz on its highest speed for a few seconds, until an emulsion has formed at the bottom. Very gradually raise the blender upwards through the ingredients until all the oil has been incorporated. Check the seasoning and the mayonnaise is ready to go. If at any time it looks like splitting (unlikely), whizz in a splash of warm water from the kettle.

Transfer to a lidded container and store in the fridge (it will keep for up to 2 weeks). Thin with a little warm water, if required, before using. This makes around 230ml (15 tablespoons) of thick mayonnaise.

Super-speedy Stick Blender Pesto Sauce

Put 50g of basil leaves (about 85g on the stem), 50g of toasted pine nuts, 50g of grated Parmesan cheese (see tip below), ½ teaspoon of salt, 2 crushed garlic cloves and 8 tablespoons (120ml) of olive oil into the beaker of a stick blender (or a tall, narrow jug or tall jam jar).

Whizz the ingredients together with the blender on its highest speed, tilting the beaker/container as necessary, until a chunky pesto has formed. If you prefer a looser consistency, simply add a little more oil.

Transfer to a sterilised jar (about 370g jam jar), cover with a slick of olive oil (to seal the pesto until required), then the lid, and store in the fridge where it will last for several weeks. It can also be frozen. This makes around 1 x 370g jar of pesto sauce.

Parmesan Cheese

Lastly, not a recipe, but this is my top tip for speeding up the oft laborious job of grating Parmesan cheese, which I find (and am constantly told) saves an enormous amount of time. I think this tip is mentioned in all of my books!

Cut a large block (or two, or more) of Parmesan into smallish chunks and grate using the grater blade of a food-processor. Remove the grater, replace with the general chopping blade and whizz until the cheese is very fine. Alternatively, you can use a hand grater or Microplane to finely grate the cheese. Store in a sealed bag in the fridge or freezer, where the cheese stays crumbly and won't set/clog up, allowing you to spoon it out and use it when required (you can use it straight from the freezer, too).

Small Plates & First Courses

This chapter includes a varied mixture of starters and slightly more substantial savoury plates, which can respectively be scaled up or down, depending on which role you have in mind for them. Alternatively, an assortment of these tasty recipes laid out in the middle of the table makes a lovely sharing lunch or light supper.

Taramasalata

SERVES 8–12

225g smoked cod's roe
2 slices white bread, crusts removed
1 garlic clove, roughly chopped
  (more if you like)
150ml vegetable oil
150ml olive oil, plus (optional)
  extra to serve
1 tablespoon fresh lemon juice
black olives, to garnish (optional)
warm pitta bread, to serve

GET AHEAD

• The taramasalata will keep
  for up to 3 days, covered,
  in the fridge.

HINTS & TIPS

• If the taramasalata is a bit of a
  sludgy beige colour (this depends
  on the colour of the roe at the outset),
  a tiny drop or two of pink or red
  food colouring can be added and
  combined while still in the processor.
  The easiest way to dispense this is
  to dip a skewer into the colouring
  and flick it in, a tiny drop at a time.
  Be careful though as it's very easy
  to overdo it! It shouldn't be anything
  like as pink as the bought processed
  taramasalata.

• Sliced smoked cod's roe on toast or
  griddled bread is delicious, too!

'Tarama' probably needs no introduction, but I will just say that when home-made, it bears no resemblance in taste or looks to the bright pink shop-bought version … there's no going back! It is great as a starter, for canapés, as a dip for crudités or as part of a meze.

1. Scrape the smoked cod's roe out of its skin and into a food-processor (discard the skin).

2. Wet the bread under a cold tap, squeeze out the excess water and add to the cod's roe, followed by the garlic. Process until smooth.

3. With the processor running, slowly and gradually add both oils as if making mayonnaise. If the mixture becomes very thick, add a little warm water from the kettle to thin it slightly. Continue until all the oil is added, then add the lemon juice.

4. Taste the taramasalata and add more oil or lemon juice to taste. Thin it to the desired consistency with warm water, if necessary. Transfer to a serving bowl or plate and garnish with black olives (if using) and a swirl of olive oil, too, if you like. Serve with warm pitta bread.

Tarragon Prawn Pots

SERVES 4

200g raw peeled prawns
(250g frozen weight), thawed
if frozen, or 5 larger raw king
prawns per person
knob of butter
150g crème fraîche (see *Hints
& Tips*)
salt and freshly ground black pepper
a small handful of tarragon leaves
(approx. 10g), a few reserved
for garnish and the remainder
chopped, or 1 teaspoon dried
tarragon, plus an extra pinch
for garnish
40g Gruyère cheese, grated
1 tablespoon breadcrumbs,
dried or fresh

A very simple, quick and tasty starter. We absolutely love this version (as does everyone) of a recipe a friend kindly gave me years ago. The sauce has been described as 'lick the bowl' good! It is rich so bear this in mind when choosing the remainder of the menu.

1. Preheat the oven to 220°C/200°C fan/gas 7.

2. Drain and then dry the prawns very well on kitchen paper. If using larger prawns, halve them horizontally so they are easier to eat. Heat the butter in a frying pan and when foaming add the prawns. Cook quickly on a high heat for a few seconds, tossing and turning, until the prawns are only just beginning to turn pink. They won't be cooked through. You may need to do this in two batches, depending on the size of the pan. Divide between four small ramekins or other ovenproof dishes.

3. Heat the crème fraîche in a small saucepan to just below boiling point, then season and stir in the chopped fresh or dried tarragon. Spoon over the prawns, dividing it evenly between the dishes. Scatter over the Gruyère and then the breadcrumbs.

4. Place the dishes on a baking sheet and bake at the top of the oven for 8 minutes until the cheese is melted and bubbling. Leave to cool for 5 or so minutes (if eaten steaming hot, they will taste of nothing), then scatter with the reserved tarragon leaves or a pinch of dried tarragon, and serve (with teaspoons).

GET AHEAD

- Make to the end of step 3 up to 2 days in advance. Cool, cover and chill. Bring back to room temperature at least 30 minutes before baking.

HINTS & TIPS

- Crème fraîche – no two brands seem to have the same properties. Waitrose 'French Crème Fraîche', Crème Fraîche d'Isigny, M&S and Tesco are brands I use for melting.

- The prawn mixture is delicious spooned over cooked rice, pasta or noodles.

- For a delicious lunch, double the quantities and enjoy with crusty bread for mopping up purposes!

Roasted Asparagus with Parmesan

SERVES 4

24 medium-sized spears of
   asparagus (see *Hints & Tips*)
a swirl or two of olive oil
sea salt flakes
Parmesan or Pecorino
   cheese shavings
1–2 tablespoons pine nuts,
   toasted (optional)

**A lovely and particularly effortless way to cook and serve asparagus as
a starter, for lunch or supper or as a side dish. For vegetarians, swap the
Parmesan for a vegetarian Italian-style hard cheese, and for vegans, omit
the cheese altogether.**

1. Preheat the oven to 200°C/180°C fan/gas 6.

2. Bend the asparagus spears near their bases between your hands, until they
snap naturally, then discard the woody ends (or use these for making soup,
if you like). Put the asparagus into an ovenproof dish large enough to take it
all in just about one layer (but it's fine if it's stacked up a little).

3. Drizzle with the olive oil and sprinkle with some salt. Turn the asparagus
over with your hands to roughly coat the stems in oil – they shouldn't be
drenched, just very lightly smeared in oil and not necessarily all over.

4. Roast at the top of the oven for 10–18 minutes or until just tender.
The cooking time will depend on the thickness of the asparagus spears.

5. Just before serving, scatter with a few cheese shavings and toasted pine
nuts (if using).

GET AHEAD

• Prepare step 2 up to a day in
advance and keep loosely
covered in the fridge.

HINTS & TIPS

• I allow 6–10 spears of asparagus
per person, depending on their
thickness, which can vary hugely
(and I prefer to buy British
asparagus when in season).
You may prefer more or less.

• If multiplying the recipe, it's better
to use two ovenproof dishes.
Alternatively, use one large shallow
roasting tin or a (lipped) baking tray
instead.

• Embellish with a little Serrano
or Parma ham draped over the
asparagus after cooking. Or, better
still, sit a few cooked asparagus
spears on slices of griddled, toasted
or baked sourdough bread rubbed
with a garlic clove, and top with
poached or soft-boiled eggs (some
Parma ham is good in there as well!)

Baked Cardamom Crab

SERVES 4 as a starter
(or serves 2 as a main course)

1 tablespoon vegetable oil
½ teaspoon ginger purée from
  a jar or tube
5 green cardamom pods, seeds
  extracted and roughly ground,
  or ½ teaspoon ground cardamom
1 garlic clove, crushed
⅛ teaspoon dried chilli flakes
4 spring onions, trimmed and
  thinly sliced diagonally
200g white crab meat, flaked
100ml double cream
2 tablespoons dried breadcrumbs
  (such as panko)
salt and freshly ground black pepper
butter, for dotting

A cracker of a recipe and yet another (of many) based on what I was taught in Sri Lanka by a local chef. I urge you to give it a go, not least because it's one of my favourite recipes and is always received with delight!

1. Preheat the oven to 220°C/200°C fan/gas 7.

2. Heat the oil in a small saucepan, add the ginger, cardamom, garlic and chilli flakes and cook on a gentle heat, stirring, for a minute or two until fragrant. Add the spring onions and cook for a further minute or two until they have softened, yet are still green. Remove from the heat.

3. Stir in the crab meat, cream, 1 tablespoon of the breadcrumbs and some seasoning – it should be very well seasoned. Spoon into a shallow, ovenproof gratin dish and fork up the top. Sprinkle with the remaining breadcrumbs and dot with a little butter.

4. Bake for 15 minutes until brown around the edges and gently bubbling. Cool for 5 minutes or so before serving.

GET AHEAD

• The recipe can be completed to the end of step 3 any time on the day, cooled, covered and chilled. Bring back to room temperature an hour before baking.

• Step 2 can be prepared up to 2 days in advance, cooled and kept covered in the fridge.

HINTS & TIPS

• Make in small individual ovenproof dishes or ramekins, if you prefer.

• This also makes a very tasty dip, served warm.

Crab, Asparagus & Parmesan Omelette

SERVES 2

6 eggs
salt and freshly ground black pepper
2 good knobs of butter
8–10 thin asparagus spears
   (or 6–8 thicker ones, halved
   lengthways), cooked
100g white crab meat, flaked
2 teaspoons grated Parmesan cheese
   (see tip on page 17), plus a little
   extra for sprinkling
1–2 tablespoons freshly chopped
   mixed herbs, such as parsley,
   chives, tarragon and mint
torn chive flowers, to garnish
   (optional)

HINTS & TIPS

- Use 2 eggs per omelette if you
  prefer, with the same quantities
  of filling ingredients.

- I prefer to buy British asparagus
  when in season.

- The filling will stretch to three
  omelettes, if required.

A glorious omelette! Two lovely spring ingredients (asparagus and crab) are combined and enveloped in luscious, softly cooked eggs – harbingers of spring themselves, too, of course.

1. Make the two omelettes, one at a time. In a jug, beat 3 of the eggs lightly with a fork and season well.

2. Melt a good knob of butter in a small (around 20cm) frying pan (preferably non-stick) on a medium heat and when foaming, add the eggs. Cook on a medium heat for a few seconds until some of the egg is set, then bring the runny egg from around the edges of the pan into the middle by drawing the set mixture (with a fish slice) into the centre, forming loose wavy folds, until most, but not all, of the egg in the middle is set. Tilting the pan will help towards the end.

3. Put half the cooked asparagus over one half of the omelette, scatter over half the crab meat, then sprinkle with 1 teaspoon of Parmesan and a good pinch of the herbs. Fold over the plain half and carefully slide the omelette onto a plate. Sprinkle with a little extra Parmesan, another good pinch of chopped herbs, a grinding of black pepper and some torn chive flowers (if using). Keep warm in the oven.

4. Wipe the pan out if necessary and repeat with the remaining ingredients to make your second omelette. Serve immediately.

Burrata with Griddled Peaches & Parma Ham

2 peaches (or nectarines), ripe
  but not squidgy, halved, stoned
  and each half cut into 4 wedges
olive oil, for drizzling
4 handfuls of mixed salad leaves
1 burrata cheese, drained
4 slices Parma ham
sea salt flakes and freshly ground
  black pepper
balsamic syrup, for drizzling

GET AHEAD

• The peaches can be griddled up
  to a day in advance, cooled,
  covered and chilled (bring back
  to room temperature to serve),
  or set aside at room temperature
  if cooked ahead on the day.

HINTS & TIPS

• Assemble the salad on one large
  platter, if you prefer.

• Balsamic syrup is sold in most
  supermarkets and lasts for ages.

Sweet, juicy, slightly caramelised peaches marry so well with rich cheese and Parma ham in this starter or lunch dish, and the sweet yet savoury umami flavour of the balsamic syrup brings it all together nicely. Short of time? Skip griddling the peaches. It's very good served with some griddled artisan bread.

1. Put the peach wedges onto a plate, drizzle over a tiny glug of olive oil and rub a little onto both sides of each wedge. Heat a dry griddle or frying pan until smoking hot, add the peach wedges, press down gently with a fish slice and cook on a high heat for around 1–2 minutes on each side, wait until they lift off willingly before turning, and are golden and a little charred (possibly a little blackened in places, too). Remove to a plate and reserve any juices from the pan.

2. Arrange the salad leaves on four plates and dot the peach wedges evenly over the leaves, nestling them in a little. Tear the burrata into bite-sized pieces and divide between the plates, then drape a slice of Parma ham, roughly torn into strips, over the top of each plate in a wavy pattern.

3. Spoon over any peach juices, sprinkle the salads with a little salt, a good grinding of black pepper and a drizzle of olive oil. Drizzle with balsamic syrup, forming zig-zag lines over the top of the salads (a thumb partly over the top of the bottle will help the syrup to come out in a thin stream) and serve immediately.

Beetroot, Goats' Cheese, Watercress & Hazelnut Salad

80g watercress
180g beetroot, cooked, cooled
   and cut into bite-sized wedges
   or batons (see *Hints & Tips*)
125g soft goats' cheese
sea salt flakes and freshly ground
   black pepper
hazelnut, walnut or olive oil,
   for drizzling
balsamic syrup, for drizzling
a small handful of whole blanched
   hazelnuts (around 30g),
   toasted and chunkily chopped
   (see *Get Ahead*)
50–60g (6 heaped teaspoons)
   fresh pomegranate seeds
roughly chopped dill, to finish
   (optional)

There are all sorts of pleasing sensations going on in this simple jewel-coloured salad – peppery, spicy watercress, creamy mild cheese, crunch from the nuts, sweet, earthy beetroot and crisp bursts of fresh fruitiness from the pomegranate seeds. Served on individual plates, it makes a lovely starter or side salad, or piled onto one platter, it makes a lovely main course salad in its own right. If you buy the beetroot ready-cooked, it is little more than an assembly job! For vegetarians, ensure the goats' cheese you use is suitable.

1. Divide the watercress between six pretty plates or shallow bowls and nestle in the beetroot. Using a teaspoon, divide the goats' cheese between the plates/bowls scattering it around in small blobs, then season each salad with salt and pepper.

2. Drizzle each plate/bowl with a little oil and some balsamic syrup, then scatter over some toasted hazelnuts, a teaspoonful of pomegranate seeds and, lastly, some dill (if using). Serve immediately.

GET AHEAD

- If cooking the beetroot, this can be done up to 3 days in advance, cooled, covered and chilled. Please see the method in *Hints & Tips*.

- The hazelnuts can be toasted up to 3 days ahead, or further ahead and frozen (no need to defrost before use). Toast the whole hazelnuts in a small, dry frying pan on a medium heat, stirring them around in the pan, until they become fragrant and light golden brown. Watch them, as once hot, they brown very quickly! Cool, then chop and keep in a covered dish.

HINTS & TIPS

- To cook beetroot, preheat the oven to 190°C/170°C fan/gas 5. Cut any leaves from the beetroot, leaving 2.5cm of stalks attached and the roots intact. Wash well, then place (unpeeled) onto a large sheet of foil, drizzle over a little olive oil, season and wrap up loosely, forming a large, airy 'tent'. Place in a roasting tin/tray and bake for 1 hour or until tender (the skins will slip off easily when cooked). When cool enough to handle, slide off the skins (wearing gloves to prevent stained hands is advisable).

- If buying ready-cooked beetroot, ensure it's plain and not infused with any flavours such as vinegar or chilli, and dry it very well on kitchen paper.

Padrón Peppers

SERVES AS MANY
AS REQUIRED

olive oil, for cooking and drizzling
fresh padrón peppers – allow 4–5
   per person as tapas, or 8–10 per
   person as a starter (around 15
   peppers = 130g)
sea salt flakes, for sprinkling

HINTS & TIPS

• To ring the changes, I like to add
  a good pinch of ground cumin
  a minute or so before the end of
  cooking and top with crumbled
  feta cheese before serving.

• Alternatively, serve as a vegetable
  to accompany grilled meat or fish.

These small peppers, traditionally served as tapas in Spain, are typically eaten with the fingers by holding on to the stem and eating the whole pepper (bar the stem). They couldn't be easier to cook, but beware, although mostly very mild, it is said that one in ten are super-hot – so the culinary version of Russian roulette! They're available from most larger supermarkets. Suitable for vegetarians and vegans.

1. Heat a little olive oil in a large frying pan and when it's very hot, add the peppers. Depending on how many peppers you are cooking and the size of the frying pan, this may need to be done in batches. Cook on a high heat for around 4–5 minutes, tossing and turning over with a fish slice from time to time, until the peppers are beginning to collapse, lose their glossy, waxy texture and are a little charred in places.

2. Transfer to a serving bowl or plate, drizzle over a little olive oil, scatter with a generous amount of salt, and serve.

Sea Bass Tartare

SERVES 4 AS A STARTER
(or serves 2 as a small plate)

3 tablespoons thick mayonnaise
(see notes on page 17)
2 tablespoons kimchi (from a jar),
drained and squeezed dry of its
liquid within the spoon, or
½ tablespoon kimchi paste
250g sea bass fillets, very fresh,
skinned and cut into ½cm dice
small pinch of dried chilli flakes
6 dill sprigs, 5 roughly chopped,
1 reserved for garnish
salt and freshly ground black pepper
squeeze of fresh lemon juice
1 x 50g jar salmon or trout roe/
caviar

GET AHEAD

• Step 1 can be completed up to
3 days in advance; keep covered
and chilled. Complete to the end
of step 2 any time on the day,
cover and chill.

Having very much enjoyed sea bass tartare in Portugal, I asked the chef about the intriguing ingredients. He kindly gave me a rough idea (the secret ingredient is kimchi mayo) and this is my interpretation. It also happens to be one of my favourite recipes in the book!

It's a simple starter (or small plate) to make, especially if you ask the fishmonger to skin the sea bass for you – although the skin's not at all difficult to remove. On the rich side, the tartare needs to be served with something very plain, such as melba toast, or the sourdough wafers I include here.

1. Whizz the mayonnaise and kimchi together using a stick blender or in a mini chopper, until smooth. If using kimchi paste, mix it with the mayonnaise in a small bowl.

2. Put the sea bass into a small mixing bowl with the kimchi mayonnaise, chilli flakes, chopped dill and some seasoning, stir to combine, check the seasoning and add a little lemon juice to taste. The mixture should be creamy, rather than runny, with the mayonnaise lightly coating the fish. Reserve a teaspoon of salmon or trout roe/caviar, and very gently stir in the remainder.

3. Arrange the tartare on four plates or wide shallow bowls and garnish with the reserved roe/caviar and fronds of dill. Serve with Crispy Sourdough Wafers (see below) or melba toast.

Crispy Sourdough Wafers

MAKES AS MANY
AS REQUIRED

sourdough, or other artisan bread

GET AHEAD

• Store in an airtight container or
wrapped in clingfilm. As the wafers
are dried out, they will last for
several weeks. Alternatively, they
can be frozen (defrost before use).

It's well worth making more of these tasty wafers than you need, as they're handy to accompany all sorts of other things. Randomly snapped into smaller wafers, they make appealing rustic bases for canapés, too. The fact that they last for a month or two in an airtight container just adds to their charm. Suitable for vegetarians and vegans.

1. Preheat the oven to 200°C/180°C fan/gas 6.

2. Slice sourdough, or other artisan bread, as thinly as you possibly can and put on a baking sheet in a single layer. Bake for 8–10 minutes (watch them!) until crisp and dried out. Transfer to a wire rack to cool. The wafers will crisp up further as they cool. Larger wafers can be roughly snapped into smaller pieces.

Saganaki

SERVES 2–3
(or serves 6 as part of a meze)

1 rectangular sheet of filo pastry
good knob of butter, melted,
    or about ½ tablespoon olive oil
    (plus extra olive oil, if frying
    the saganaki)
1 x 200g block of feta cheese
    (see intro), drained and
    blotted dry
good pinch of dried oregano
poppy seeds, for sprinkling
    (if baking the saganaki)
1–2 tablespoons runny honey
    (more if you like)
dried chilli flakes, to taste
toasted black and white sesame
    seeds, for sprinkling (see *Hints
    & Tips*)
thyme sprigs and/or lemon wedges,
    to garnish (optional)

GET AHEAD

• Complete to the end of step 3 up to
  a day ahead, cover and chill. Bring
  back to room temperature for an
  hour before cooking.

HINTS & TIPS

• To toast sesame seeds, cook them in
  a small, dry frying pan on a medium
  heat, stirring continuously, until they
  become fragrant and light golden
  brown. Be alert, as this happens
  very quickly! I find it useful to toast
  more sesame seeds than I need, then
  cool and freeze the extra for future
  use (just use from frozen).

This is my version of this lovely rustic Cretan dish – soft, warm feta cheese, crisp filo pastry and sweet honey. Enjoy it as part of a meze, or as is with a salad or two.

Look for feta cheese that carries the round red and yellow PDO logo. Brands without this are best avoided. Fry the Saganaki, or bake in the oven, it's up to you. For vegetarians, ensure the feta you use is suitable.

1. If baking the saganaki, preheat the oven to 200°C/180°C fan/gas 6 and line a baking sheet with baking parchment or silicone paper.

2. Lay the sheet of filo pastry out with the shortest edge closest to you (portrait) and immediately brush it with some melted butter or olive oil.

3. Place the cheese lengthways in the middle of the pastry, roughly 5cm up from the bottom, and sprinkle with a good pinch of dried oregano. Wrap the cheese in the pastry, folding over and upwards from the bottom, twice. Now fold in the excess pastry on both sides to envelop the cheese, and then continue folding the cheese up and over the remainder of the pastry to form a neatish parcel/envelope. Don't worry if it's not as neat as a perfectly wrapped present.

4. If baking, put the cheese parcel onto the lined baking sheet with the seams underneath. Brush well with melted butter or olive oil and sprinkle with poppy seeds. Bake for 20 minutes or until golden brown and crisp. If frying, skip the poppy seeds. Heat a good glug of olive oil in a small frying pan and cook the cheese parcel on a medium heat until golden brown, about 4 minutes on each side.

5. Transfer the baked or fried cheese to a serving plate or dish and serve immediately, drizzled with the honey, sprinkled with a few chilli flakes and toasted sesame seeds and garnished with some thyme sprigs and/or lemon wedges, if you like.

• It matters not how you wrap the
  cheese in the filo, just as long as it's
  enclosed, as in an envelope!

• The unused filo pastry can be frozen
  (or kept frozen), if necessary.

• Tomato and cucumber salad with
  a little sliced or chopped red onion
  is a very good accompaniment,
  as is the Tomato & Chilli Salad
  (see page 167) and a green salad.

Green Vegetable Medley
with Burrata & Hazelnuts

SERVES 6 as a starter
(or serves 4 as a main course)

100g sugar snap peas, topped,
    tailed, stringy bits removed
    (or use mangetout or whole
    tender young pea pods)
salt
100g podded edamame beans,
    fresh or frozen
100g peas, freshly podded
    or frozen
2 burrata cheeses, drained
2 oregano sprigs, leaves picked,
    or a good pinch of dried oregano
sea salt flakes and freshly ground
    black pepper
olive oil, for drizzling
50g blanched whole hazelnuts,
    toasted and chunkily chopped
    (see *Get Ahead* tip on page 35)
3 mint sprigs, leaves picked and
    roughly chopped

To finish (optional)
pea shoots; micro leaves; salad
    cress; edible flowers such as
    borage or violas

A delightful melange of green veggies, sitting on a bed of creamy white burrata, topped with toasted hazelnuts. Crisp and crunchy, yet soft, fresh and vibrant, this colourful salad is positively bursting with different textures. For vegetarians, ensure the burratas you use are suitable.

1. Put the sugar snap peas into a small saucepan with a good pinch of salt, barely cover with boiling water and simmer for 3–5 minutes until just tender. Drain and cool immediately under cold running water. Roll up in kitchen paper to dry. Repeat the process with the edamame beans and peas, cooking them together in the same pan for 3 minutes, then drain, cool and dry as before. If using frozen peas, add them to the edamame beans after 3 minutes, quickly bring back to the boil and drain immediately.

2. Break the burrata into pieces and spread out over the base of a large serving plate or dish, then sprinkle with the oregano. Scatter over the mixed vegetables, leaving a margin of burrata showing around the edge. Season generously with salt flakes and pepper, then drizzle with a little olive oil and scatter over the hazelnuts and mint. Finish with a little more olive oil and any of the suggestions (if using) and serve immediately.

GET AHEAD

- Step 1 can be completed up to
  a day in advance. Wrap the
  vegetables, still rolled in their kitchen
  paper, in clingfilm and chill. Bring
  back to room temperature to serve.

- The hazelnuts can be toasted up to
  3 days ahead, or further ahead and
  frozen.

HINTS & TIPS

- Just before serving, sprinkle the
  salad with 1–2 teaspoons of ground
  sumac for a delicious lemony hit.

- Almost any green vegetables
  can be used. Try broad beans
  (double podded), asparagus, baby
  courgettes, tenderstem or purple
  sprouting broccoli.

- The hazelnuts can be swapped for
  pine nuts or (shelled) pistachios.

Smoked Salmon with Fennel & Red Onion Pickles

SERVES 4

1 small fennel bulb, tough outer
    layer and stems discarded, thinly
    sliced (I use a mandolin) and
    fronds reserved
1 small red onion, halved through
    the root and thinly sliced (I use
    a mandolin)
good pinch of fennel seeds,
    roughly crushed
good pinch of both black and
    white mustard seeds
250g thin smoked salmon slices

For the pickling liquid
8 tablespoons (120ml) white wine
    vinegar
4 tablespoons granulated sugar
1 teaspoon salt

To finish
reserved fennel fronds (or dill, if
    making the fennel pickle more
    than 3 days in advance); snipped
    chives; salad cress; micro or rocket
    leaves; small capers or caperberries;
    a grinding of black pepper

Ever-popular smoked salmon is jazzed up here with some quick pickles, which cut through the richness of the salmon brilliantly. Do buy the best quality smoked salmon you can. Everything can be prepared well in advance, leaving hardly anything to do before serving. Dress the plates up as much as you like, or just keep them simple. You won't need all the pickles, but they keep for ages in the fridge and have many other uses.

1. Place the fennel and red onion in two separate small bowls or jars, into which they only just fit. Add the fennel and mustard seeds to the fennel bowl.

2. To make the pickling liquid, put the vinegar, sugar and salt into a small saucepan, stir on a low heat for a minute or so to dissolve, then bring to the boil and bubble for 1 minute. Pour half of this over the fennel and the other half over the onion. Set aside, ideally for 2 hours, but the pickles can be used after 1 hour. Cover when cool and store in the fridge.

3. Divide the smoked salmon between four plates in an undulating, wavy pattern.

4. Arrange a small teaspoonful of both pickles (drained of their pickling liquid by pressing the teaspoon against the edge of the bowl or jar) on each plate. Finish with any/some of the suggestions and serve.

GET AHEAD

- Steps 1 and 2 can be prepared several weeks in advance and chilled, although pickles will keep for several months in the fridge.

- Step 3 can be completed any time on the day, covered and kept somewhere cool.

HINTS & TIPS

- Pickled onion loses the astringency (unpalatable for some) of raw onion.

Roasted Harissa Tomatoes & Red Peppers with Chickpeas, Yoghurt & Mint

SERVES 4

300g cherry tomatoes
3 large whole roasted red peppers
   from a jar, drained and torn into
   long strips
2 teaspoons rose harissa paste
generous pinch of dried oregano
sea salt flakes and freshly ground
   black pepper
olive oil, for drizzling
500g strained Greek yoghurt
1 x 400g tin or jar chickpeas,
   drained, rinsed and dried on
   kitchen paper
a small handful of mint leaves,
   chopped
a small handful of coriander,
   roughly chopped
nigella or onion seeds, for scattering
   (optional)
crusty bread or warm pittas or
   flatbreads, to serve

Pleasingly quick to prepare, this tasty dish can be put together in a jiffy. Spicy roasted tomatoes and peppers contrast beautifully with luscious, thick, creamy yoghurt, crunchy chickpeas and fresh mint. It's important to use strained Greek yoghurt in this recipe, which is thicker than regular Greek-style yoghurt. Suitable for vegetarians.

1. Preheat the oven to 220°C/200°C fan/gas 7.

2. Put the tomatoes, peppers, harissa paste, oregano and some salt and pepper into a shallow roasting tin (approx. 20 x 26cm) with a generous glug of olive oil. Swish everything around until coated, then shake the tin so the ingredients are spread out in (roughly) one layer. Bake at the top of the oven for 15 minutes, until the tomatoes have collapsed but are still holding their shape. Check the seasoning, then set aside to cool. The sauce will thicken up a little as it cools and the tomato mixture should be served at room temperature.

3. Spread the yoghurt out on a large serving plate (roughly 30cm) or dish, then spoon the tomato mixture over the top, leaving a margin of yoghurt showing around the edge. Gently nestle the chickpeas into the tomatoes. Scatter over the herbs and some nigella or onion seeds, finish with a generous swirl of olive oil and serve with crusty bread or warm pittas or flatbreads for scooping. A green salad would be good, too.

GET AHEAD

• Step 2 can be completed up to 3 days ahead, cooled, covered and chilled. Bring back to room temperature to serve. If cooked earlier on the day of eating, leave in the tin at room temperature until required.

HINTS & TIPS

• This is a delicious accompaniment to lamb, chicken and barbecued meat, or as a salad.

• In the absence of strained yoghurt, strain regular thick Greek-style yoghurt in a sieve lined with (damp) muslin, over a bowl. Cover and chill overnight, then use as required the next day.

Things on Toast

Tartines, open sandwiches, call them what you will, you'll find a mixture of inviting savoury and sweet recipes in this chapter (one of my favourite chapters in the book). The variations are as wide and flexible as your imagination. Use these recipes as a rough guide and for inspiration, then do your own thing according to what you have available, bearing in mind that an egg, some quick pickles, dried chilli flakes or Aleppo pepper (pul biber) rarely go amiss.

Most of these recipes make four average slices of toast with topping, but as slices come in different sizes you may wish to make more, depending on how many and who you're feeding. I recommend basing toppings on what you have in the fridge and store cupboard and taking it from there. A jar of zhoug lasts for ages in the fridge, as do quick pickles (and they are so fast to make). Armed with a stock of these, you will have plenty of scope for zinging up whatever's underneath. Roasted Garlic (see page 60) needs to be made in advance and keeps for weeks in the fridge, so it's worth roasting several bulbs together, ready to use with other things as well.

These recipes are very relaxed, just a guide really, so stack up the toasts, however you like … or set up a pick 'n' mix so everyone can build their own. They are the theme for many of our lunches at home as well as for supper on Sunday evenings.

Kimchi, Avocado & Cheese Melts

MAKES 4 MELTS

4 slices sourdough bread (I like
  seeded or wholemeal sourdough)
butter, for spreading
1 ripe avocado, halved and stoned
8 teaspoons kimchi (from a jar),
  drained of its liquid on the spoon
salt and freshly ground black pepper
100g Taleggio cheese, thinly sliced,
  including the rind
parsley or rocket leaves (optional)
olive oil, for drizzling

HINTS & TIPS

• For vegetarians, swap grated
  vegetarian Cheddar cheese for
  the Taleggio. It won't be as creamy,
  but will be delicious all the same.

Kimchi could be described as the Korean version of sauerkraut and, as with all things fermented, it aids a healthy digestive system. It's readily available in jars from supermarkets. As always with grilling, the grill needs to be fully preheated on its hottest setting for the best results. This makes a very flavourful slice of toast.

1. Preheat the grill to its highest setting.

2. Toast the sourdough and spread with butter. Using a round-bladed knife, cut the avocado into long, thin slices within its skin. Using a spoon, scoop out a quarter of these slices at a time and arrange them over each slice of toast. Repeat for the remaining three toast slices. Top the avocado with the drained kimchi, season, then arrange the cheese on top, breaking it up as necessary.

3. Put onto a baking sheet and cook at the top of the grill for 4–5 minutes, until the cheese has melted and is beginning to brown around the edges.

4. Leave to cool for a few minutes before serving (while steaming hot, it will taste of nothing), then scatter with the parsley or rocket leaves (if using) and finish each slice with a grinding of black pepper and a swirl of olive oil.

Spicy Crab 'Rarebits'

MAKES 4 RAREBITS

100g white crab meat, flaked

3 teaspoons Dijon mustard

2 tablespoons thick mayonnaise
  (see my notes on page 17)

1 tablespoon double cream

a few drops of Worcestershire sauce,
  or to taste

a few drops of Tabasco sauce,
  or a pinch of dried chilli flakes,
  or to taste

2 spring onions, trimmed and
  chopped (see *Hints & Tips*)

3 tablespoons grated Parmesan
  or Pecorino cheese (see tip
  on page 17)

salt and freshly ground black pepper

4 slices sourdough (I like seeded
  or wholemeal sourdough) or
  artisan-style bread (or more,
  if slices are small)

butter, for spreading

4 slices pickled jalapeños from
  a jar, drained (optional)

a small bunch of chives, snipped,
  to garnish

Not strictly a rarebit, but without the need to make a sauce and therefore requiring far less effort, this recipe achieves a similar creamy, cheesy result. This tops four generous-sized slices of toast, or more smaller ones. Cut into small squares, this makes extremely tasty canapés. It's possibly our favourite Sunday night supper – highly recommended!

1. Preheat the grill to its highest setting.

2. In a small bowl, mix all the ingredients together, except the bread, butter, jalapeños (if using) and chives. Check for flavour and seasoning and adjust accordingly. The mixture should be quite spicy and very well seasoned.

3. Toast the bread and spread with butter, then put on a baking sheet (lined with baking parchment or silicone paper, if you like). Top with the crab mixture and spread to the edges. Finish each with a slice of jalapeño (if using) and cook at the top of the hot grill until golden and bubbling, about 3–5 minutes, but watch them!

4. Leave to cool for 5 minutes or so before scattering with the chives and serving.

GET AHEAD

- Step 2 can be prepared any time on the day, covered and chilled.

HINTS & TIPS

- The easiest way to chop spring onions is to quarter them lengthways, gather together, then chop at right angles into small pieces.

- Although delicious on its own, watercress or chicory (or a salad of both together), lightly dressed, is a lovely accompaniment, as are sliced radishes.

- Sometimes I like to add some chicory, quartered lengthways (and/or radicchio), rubbed with a little olive oil and sprinkled with sea salt flakes, to the baking sheet alongside the toasts, to grill until softened and charred.

1. KIMCHI, AVOCADO &
CHEESE MELTS

2. SPICY CRAB 'RAREBITS'

1. JAMMY TOMATOES ON SOURDOUGH TOASTS

2. CREAMY MUSHROOM & TARRAGON TOASTS

3. KIPPERED EGGS

Jammy Tomatoes on Sourdough Toast

MAKES 4 SLICES OF TOAST

a small splash of olive oil
20g butter, plus extra for spreading
500g tomatoes, quartered,
   each quarter cut into chunks
salt and freshly ground black pepper
4–6 slices sourdough bread (I like
   seeded or wholemeal sourdough)

GET AHEAD

• The tomatoes can be cooked,
   cooled, covered and stored in the
   fridge for up to 3 days (or a little
   longer), or frozen (defrost before
   use). Reheat gently in a pan until hot
   throughout.

HINTS & TIPS

• Add some freshly chopped herbs
   and/or crushed/chopped garlic,
   if you like.

• Topping suggestions: a poached,
   fried or 6½-minute soft-boiled egg;
   anchovy fillets in oil (drained);
   sliced avocado; dried chilli flakes;
   a grinding of black pepper; basil
   or rocket leaves.

You can't beat tomatoes cooked down to a pulpy paste, which greatly intensifies and deepens their flavour. I make this with home-grown tomatoes in summer, and it's a great way to enhance the taste of watery shop-bought tomatoes the rest of the year. We usually have a tomato surplus, so I make big batches and freeze in small containers to enjoy until the tomato season comes around again.

Suitable for vegans (omitting the butter) and vegetarians, the tomatoes can be used to add flavour to myriad other dishes as well – a spoonful in scrambled eggs (added with the butter at the beginning) is a favourite.

1. Heat the olive oil and butter in a saucepan (a deep-sided one helps to reduce splattering). Add the tomatoes and some seasoning (they do need to be generously seasoned) and cook fast on a high heat, stirring from time to time, until the tomatoes become pulpy and just about all the liquid has been driven off. The tomatoes are ready when the mixture doesn't fill back in after a wooden spoon is drawn through the middle of the pulp in the pan. This will take between 5–10 minutes but will depend on the water content of the tomatoes and the time of year. The higher the heat, the speedier this will be.

2. While the tomatoes are cooking, toast and butter the bread and keep warm.

3. Spread the tomatoes over the toast and serve as is, or with toppings of your choice (see *Hints & Tips*).

Creamy Mushroom & Tarragon Toasts

MAKES 4 SLICES OF TOAST

a small splash of olive oil
30g butter, plus extra for spreading
1 shallot, finely chopped
1 garlic clove, crushed
4 tarragon sprigs, leaves of 3 roughly
    chopped, or ½ teaspoon dried
    tarragon, plus an extra pinch
    to serve
300–350g mixed mushrooms
    (such as chestnut, shiitake,
    oyster, wild), some sliced,
    remainder quartered
salt and freshly ground black pepper
4 tablespoons dry sherry or Marsala
2 tablespoons crème fraîche
    (more if you like)
a squeeze of fresh lemon juice
    (optional)
4 slices sourdough (I like seeded
    or wholemeal sourdough),
    4 individual brioche rolls, halved,
    or 4 slices from a brioche loaf

Enjoy these tasty mushrooms for a vegetarian lunch, supper or snack. If using any wild mushrooms in the mix, do ensure they're reliably sourced. Up the ante with a few drops of truffle oil before serving, if you have it. Suitable for vegetarians.

1. Heat the oil and butter in a medium saucepan and cook the shallot on a low heat for a few minutes until beginning to soften. Add the garlic, chopped fresh or dried tarragon, mushrooms and some seasoning, then cook on a high heat, stirring, until any moisture has evaporated and the mushrooms begin to sizzle. Add the sherry or Marsala and cook fast until the liquid has reduced to around one tablespoon. Stir in the crème fraîche and bring to a simmer. Check the seasoning and add a little lemon juice, if you like.

2. Toast the sourdough bread or brioche (brioche burns very quickly due to its sugar content, so beware and toast it very lightly), spread with butter and put on individual plates.

3. Spoon the mushroom mixture over the toasts, garnish with the leaves from the last sprig of tarragon, or sprinkle with a pinch of dried tarragon, and serve.

GET AHEAD

• Step 1 can be completed up to
  2 days in advance, cooled, covered
  and chilled. Reheat gently before
  continuing as above.

HINTS & TIPS

• The crème fraîche will glaze the
  mushrooms, rather than form a runny
  sauce. If you prefer, add a little more
  crème fraîche or water for a creamier,
  thinner sauce.

Kippered Eggs

MAKES 4 SLICES OF TOAST

1 pair kipper fillets (approximately
   200g), the skin pulled off
4 slices sourdough bread (I like
   seeded or wholemeal sourdough)
good knob of butter, plus extra
   for spreading
8 eggs
salt and freshly ground black pepper
a few parsley sprigs, to garnish

GET AHEAD

• Step 1 can be completed
  up to 3 days in advance.
  Keep covered in the fridge.

HINTS & TIPS

• To ensure big curds and a lovely
  texture when scrambling eggs,
  don't add any salt until the last
  minute. Be judicious with salt in
  this recipe as kippers are salty.

• If making for fewer people, any
  leftover kipper fillet can be frozen.

A tasty combination from times gone by, but definitely no less wonderful for that! It goes without saying, this is just the job for breakfast or brunch, but I happily eat it for lunch or supper, too. The advantage of kipper fillets, as opposed to whole kippers, is that the residual bones are so fine, they can be ignored and eaten without any concern. However, you might like to pull some of them out if they appear while breaking up the fillets. This is rich so I have allowed two eggs per person, but you may like to add more.

1. Break each kipper fillet in half lengthways through the natural divide down the middle, then gently tear each of the strips into bite-sized chunks.

2. Toast the bread and spread with butter, then keep warm.

3. Melt the knob of butter in a small (preferably non-stick) saucepan on a low heat. Remove from the heat, cool down a little, then break the eggs into the saucepan and scramble/break them up with a wooden spoon. Add some black pepper, put back on a low heat and stir continuously until partially but not completely set. Remove from the heat, add a little salt and gently stir in the kipper chunks, without breaking them up. By this time, the eggs will most likely have cooked to your liking in the residual heat of the pan. If not, stir on a low heat for another minute.

4. Divide the scrambled eggs between the slices of toast, garnish with some parsley sprigs and serve immediately.

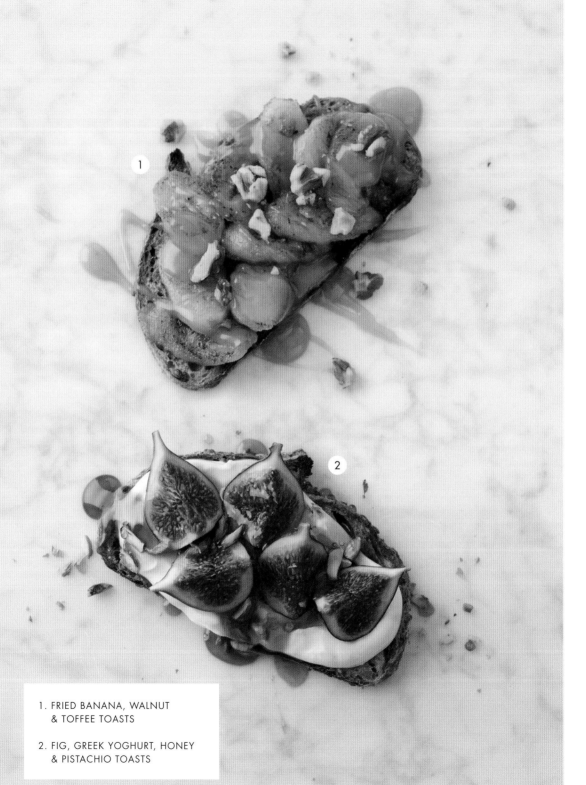

1. FRIED BANANA, WALNUT
   & TOFFEE TOASTS

2. FIG, GREEK YOGHURT, HONEY
   & PISTACHIO TOASTS

Fried Banana, Walnut & Toffee Toasts

MAKES 2 SLICES OF TOAST

2 slices sourdough bread
(I like seeded or wholemeal
sourdough)
30g butter
2 firm bananas, cut into 1.5cm
diagonal wedges, or halve
lengthways if you prefer
4 teaspoons demerara sugar
4 tablespoons double cream
1 tablespoon walnut pieces

Great for breakfast with a dollop of yoghurt, as a snack or for pudding, this is sticky, caramelised and thoroughly indulgent! Skip the toast if you like, and serve in little bowls. Suitable for vegetarians.

1. Toast the bread and keep warm on two plates.

2. Melt the butter in a small frying pan on a medium heat and when foaming, add the bananas, cut-side down. Turn over when golden underneath, about 2–3 minutes, and cook for another minute or so. The bananas should have softened and be slightly collapsing around the edges, but still holding their shape. Divide the bananas between the toast.

3. Off the heat, add the sugar and cream to the pan. Return to a low heat and stir gently for a minute or two until the mixture bubbles up into a thick, smooth and pale fudge-coloured toffee sauce. Spoon over the bananas and top with the walnuts. Leave for a few minutes before serving – the mixture will be burning hot and will taste of nothing until it cools down a little.

Fig, Greek Yoghurt, Honey & Pistachio Toasts

MAKES 4 SLICES OF TOAST

4 slices white sourdough bread
butter, for spreading
around 4 tablespoons thick Greek-
style yoghurt, cold from the fridge
4 ripe fresh figs (use 6, if small),
quartered or thinly sliced
4 teaspoons clear honey
4 small pieces of honeycomb
(optional)
1 tablespoon unsalted (shelled)
pistachio nuts, cut into slivers
or roughly chopped

To garnish
dried rose petals; thyme sprigs;
edible flowers (optional)

Breakfast, a pudding or a snack – it's up to you! Fresh, sweet and creamy with a little bit of crunch, these are surprisingly good for something so easy and simple. Swapping the yoghurt for goats' curd, or soft or hard goats' cheese, adapts the toasts into a tasty savoury-sweet concoction. Suitable for vegetarians.

1. Toast the sourdough and spread with butter.

2. Spoon some yoghurt onto each slice and arrange the figs on top. Drizzle over the honey, top each slice with a piece of honeycomb (if using) and scatter with the pistachios. Garnish with any of the suggestions and serve immediately.

HINTS & TIPS

• Other ripe soft fruits or berries, such as peaches, nectarines, apricots, cherries (stoned), strawberries and raspberries, make a nice alternative to the figs.

Roasted Garlic, Avocado, Parma Ham & Sun-dried Tomato Bruschetta

MAKES 4 BRUSCHETTA

4 slices sourdough bread (I like
  seeded or wholemeal sourdough)
butter, for spreading
1 Roasted Garlic bulb (around
  3 cloves per slice are required) –
  see recipe below
1 small ripe avocado, halved,
  stoned and sliced in its skin
salt and freshly ground black pepper
4 small handfuls of rocket leaves
4 slices Parma ham
4 sun-dried tomatoes, torn into
  chunky strips (use the sun-dried
  ones in oil, drained, or the semi-
  dried ones)
1 tablespoon pine nuts, toasted
olive oil, for drizzling
basil leaves, to garnish

Combining flavours from Italy gives these toasts an Italian theme. Roasted garlic is a lovely thing when spread on toast, and indeed for all sorts of other uses. Make it in advance and keep a stash in the fridge.

1. Toast the bread and spread with butter.

2. Spread 3 cloves of roasted garlic onto each slice of toast. Equally divide the slices of avocado between the toast, and season. Top each slice with a small handful of rocket leaves, followed by a slice of Parma ham, arranged in a wavy pattern, some sun-dried tomato strips and pine nuts. Lastly, drizzle with a little olive oil and scatter with a few basil leaves. Serve.

Roasted Garlic

MAKES 1 ROASTED BULB

1 garlic bulb (or more)
salt
olive oil

GET AHEAD

• Squeeze the garlic paste out of
  each roasted clove individually into
  a ramekin or clean jar, submerge
  in a little olive oil, cover and store
  in the fridge. Or, squeeze from the
  whole bulb, mix into a paste with
  a little olive oil, cover and store
  in the fridge, where the garlic will
  last for several weeks.

Roasted garlic needs to be cooked in advance for this recipe. It only takes around 30 minutes to cook and keeps for weeks in the fridge, so it's well worth roasting several bulbs at a time, ready to use with other things as well. Roasting takes away the raw astringency, transforming the garlic into a soft, mellow paste. Suitable for vegetarians and vegans.

1. Preheat the oven to 200°C/180°C fan/gas 6.

2. If necessary, slice the thinnest sliver from the root end of the garlic bulb so that it sits upright. Cut a thin slice off the top of the bulb, just enough to reveal the cloves, and discard this.

3. Sit the bulb on a sheet of foil and sprinkle with a little salt and olive oil. Bring up the sides of the foil, forming a loose airtight tent around the garlic. Place on a baking sheet and roast for 35 minutes or until the cloves are soft throughout. Leave to cool to lukewarm in the foil parcel before squeezing out the garlic paste.

1. ROASTED GARLIC, AVOCADO,
   PARMA HAM & SUN-DRIED
   TOMATO BRUSCHETTA

2. HAM, EGG & ANCHOVY TARTINES

Ham, Egg & Anchovy Tartines

MAKES 4 TARTINES

4 slices sourdough bread (I like
    seeded or wholemeal sourdough)
butter, for spreading
4 small handfuls of rocket leaves
100g pulled/shredded cooked
    ham hock
1 celery stick, stringy bits
    removed with a potato peeler
    and thinly sliced
2 eggs, boiled for 7 minutes,
    cooled and peeled
3 tablespoons Wasabi Watercress
    Mayonnaise (see page 63)
    (see also *Hints & Tips*)
4 anchovy fillets in oil, drained
dried chilli flakes, to taste
freshly chopped parsley, snipped
    chives, salad cress or micro
    leaves, to finish (optional)

Everyday ingredients make up these tartines, but to very tasty effect. Use any cooked ham you have to hand – it doesn't have to be pulled ham or ham hock. The celery injects a nice bit of crunch, too. (See image on page 61).

1. Toast the sourdough and spread with butter.

2. Divide the rocket leaves between the slices and then repeat with the ham hock and celery.

3. Halve the eggs, cut each half into rough chunks and arrange these on top, then spoon over the mayonnaise.

4. Top each slice with an anchovy, a pinch of chilli flakes and a scattering of any of, or a selection of, the herbs or leaves (if using), and serve.

HINTS & TIPS

- Swap the Wasabi Watercress Mayonnaise for 3 tablespoons of thick mayonnaise (see notes on page 17) combined with 1 tablespoon of whole grain (seedy) mustard. The mustard mayonnaise can be made up to 3 days in advance, covered and chilled (although it will last for longer).

- The eggs can be cooked up to 3 days in advance, cooled, peeled, submerged in a bowl of cold water, covered and chilled.

- A few Quick Pickled Red Onions (see page 65) in place of the anchovies are delicious.

Smoked Salmon & Soft-boiled Egg Tartines with Wasabi Watercress Mayonnaise

MAKES 4 TARTINES

4 eggs
4 tablespoons thick mayonnaise
  (see notes on page 17)
1½–2 teaspoons wasabi paste
50g watercress
4 slices sourdough bread (I like
  seeded or wholemeal sourdough)
butter, for spreading
4 slices smoked salmon (around
  200g in total)
salt and freshly ground black pepper

To garnish (suggestions)
snipped chives; 1 thinly sliced spring
  onion; freshly chopped dill; capers;
  dried chilli flakes; a grinding of
  black pepper; grated lemon zest;
  micro leaves

Smoked salmon and eggs are two ingredients that marry together so well, and when finished off with slightly hot and spicy, peppery wasabi and watercress mayo, they create these very tasty treats indeed. The mayonnaise is good with so many other things, including cooked fish, chicken, steak or new potatoes, egg mayonnaise … (See image on page 64).

1. Lower the eggs into a small saucepan of boiling water and simmer for 6½ minutes. Drain and leave under cold running water just until cool enough to handle (less than a minute) and then peel. Set aside.

2. While the eggs are cooking, whizz together the mayonnaise, wasabi and 30g of the watercress using a stick blender or small food-processor, until combined (or finely chop the watercress and mix with the mayo and wasabi by hand in a small bowl). Add more wasabi to taste and thin with a little warm water, if necessary.

3. Toast the sourdough and spread with butter.

4. Divide the remaining watercress between the slices of toast, followed by a slice of smoked salmon, arranged in a wavy pattern. Halve the eggs and sit two halves, cut-side up, on top of the smoked salmon on each slice. Season the eggs.

5. Spoon over the mayonnaise and finish the tartines with any of, or a mixture of, the garnish suggestions.

GET AHEAD

• The eggs are just as good served cold, in which case they can be cooked up to 3 days in advance. Submerge the peeled eggs in cold water in a small bowl, cover and chill.

• The mayonnaise can be made up to 3 days in advance, covered and chilled (although it will last longer).

HINTS & TIPS

• For a variation, switch the smoked salmon for two small hot-smoked or (cooked) fresh salmon fillets, and the soft-boiled eggs for poached eggs.

1. SMOKED SALMON & SOFT-BOILED EGG TARTINES
   WITH WASABI WATERCRESS MAYONNAISE

2. SMOKED MACKEREL WITH QUICK PICKLED
   RED ONIONS & ZHOUG

Smoked Mackerel with Quick Pickled Red Onions & Zhoug

MAKES 4 SLICES OF TOAST

4 slices sourdough bread (I like
seeded or wholemeal sourdough)
butter, for spreading
2 smoked mackerel fillets,
skin and any bones from
down the middle removed
4–8 teaspoons thick Greek-style
yoghurt
4–8 teaspoons Quick Pickled
Red Onions (see recipe below),
drained (with the spoon pressed
against the side of the jar)
4–8 teaspoons zhoug
nigella or onion seeds, for sprinkling
freshly ground black pepper
4 parsley or coriander sprigs,
to garnish (optional)

Zhoug is an extremely flavourful, hot Yemeni sauce made from coriander, chilli, garlic and spices, available ready-made in jars from Middle Eastern shops or large supermarkets. In this recipe, it cuts through the richness of the smoked mackerel and is very good stirred through all manner of other things, too.

There's a flavour-bomb happening on these slices of toast – super-savoury smoky mackerel, sweet and sour pickled onions, zingy hot and spicy zhoug, and cooling yoghurt. A very tasty treat indeed.

The quick pickled onions need to be made a minimum of 1–2 hours in advance. You will have some left over, but they have many uses and keep well.

1. Toast the sourdough and spread with butter.

2. Break the smoked mackerel fillets into pieces. Equally divide the mackerel pieces between the slices of toast and top each slice with 1–2 teaspoons of yoghurt and 1–2 teaspoons of quick pickled red onions. Dot over 1–2 teaspoons of zhoug, then scatter with nigella or onion seeds and a grinding of black pepper. Garnish with the herb sprigs (if using), and serve.

Quick Pickled Red Onions

SERVES 4–6 as an
accompaniment or topping

4 tablespoons white wine vinegar
2 tablespoons granulated sugar
½ teaspoon salt
1 red onion, halved and very
thinly sliced (I use a mandolin)

Quick pickles can be used almost as soon as they're made, but I think are better made at least 2 hours in advance (the indigestible edge of raw onion is removed when pickled). Suitable for vegetarians and vegans.

1. Put the vinegar, sugar and salt into a small saucepan, stir on a low heat for a minute or so to dissolve, then bring to the boil and bubble for 1 minute.

2. Put the red onion into the smallest bowl or jar it will fit into, then pour over the hot pickling liquid. Set aside, ideally for 2 hours, but the pickles can be used after 1 hour. Cover when cool and store in the fridge for several weeks.

GET AHEAD

• Make these quick pickles a few days in advance (although they will keep for weeks longer), then cool, cover and chill.

HINTS & TIPS

• Press a teaspoonful of the pickled onions against the edge of the bowl or jar to drain them of their pickling liquid.

• Quick pickled onions last for weeks in a covered bowl or jar in the fridge, and are very handy as a topping for all sorts of combinations on toast, salads and many other things.

Flash in the Pan Suppers

Super-quick suppers (or lunches) all cooked on the stove. These recipes are your friends when you have little time to spare and need to get tasty food on the table quickly.

You will find a wide range of delicious crowd-pleasing dishes here, so I hope there's something for everyone in this chapter, and for all ages.

Most of the recipes in the following chapter 'Bowl Food from Around the World', fall into the quick suppers (or lunches) category, too, so do check them out as well.

Meatballs in Mustard Sauce

SERVES 2–3

small glug of olive oil
1 x 300–350g packet (12 meatballs,
   sometimes more) fresh beef or
   pork meatballs
1 tablespoon Dijon mustard
1 tablespoon whole grain (seedy)
   mustard
1 teaspoon dark soy sauce
150ml chicken stock (or use
   ½ stock cube)
4 tablespoons crème fraîche
2 spring onions, trimmed and
   thinly sliced on a deep diagonal

GET AHEAD

• The recipe can be made up to 3
  days in advance, cooled, covered
  and chilled, then reheated gently
  in a pan until hot throughout,
  when required. You may need to
  loosen the sauce with a little water.

Pre-prepared meatballs make this a very speedy recipe, but by all means make your own if you prefer. Sausagemeat balls would probably be the quickest – simply slit the skins of your favourite sausages and form the meat into balls with wet hands.

1. Heat the olive oil in a small frying pan, add the meatballs and fry on a medium-high heat until well browned all over, turning with tongs, about 8–10 minutes. Drain off (and discard) most of the fat with a spoon.

2. Add both mustards, the soy sauce and stock to the pan. Bring to the boil and simmer gently for around 5 minutes, until the sauce has thickened slightly and become a little syrupy.

3. Stir in the crème fraîche and simmer, just to heat through. Scatter with the spring onions and serve with mashed or new potatoes, cooked pasta (such as pappardelle) or rice.

Buttery Plaice with Brown Shrimps, Capers & Lemon

SERVES 2

2 fillets of plaice, about 160–200g
  each, skin on or off (skin-on is
  easier to deal with and soft and
  delicious to eat)
a little plain flour, for dusting
salt
3 tablespoons butter
100g cooked peeled brown shrimps
2 heaped teaspoons capers
  in brine, drained and dried
  on kitchen paper
a handful of parsley, tough stems
  removed and roughly chopped
1 lemon

HINTS & TIPS

• Try using other white fish fillets,
  such as haddock, cod, hake or
  whiting, instead of the plaice.

• Use ready-made potted shrimps
  if you prefer, although this is a
  more expensive option.

I love the soft delicate texture of plaice. With its mild, sweet flavour, enhanced here by potted shrimps and fried capers, this is a much-enjoyed supper the day the fishmonger has called. I think petit pois and plaice complement each other beautifully, not to mention their mutual affinity with butter, which also goes for new potatoes, so these would finish this dish off perfectly.

1. Put the plaice fillets onto a plate and lightly dust both sides with a little flour and a sprinkling of salt.

2. In a frying pan large enough to hold the fillets side-by-side, heat 1 tablespoon of butter until foaming. Add the plaice, skin-side uppermost, and cook on a medium heat for around 2–3 minutes until light golden. Carefully turn over with a fish slice and cook for another 2 minutes, until just cooked through. Transfer to two (warmed) plates.

3. Add another tablespoon of butter to the pan, melt on a low heat, then add the shrimps. Remove from the heat, swirl the shrimps around in the butter, just to warm them through, then spoon the shrimps and butter over the plaice.

4. Melt the last tablespoon of butter in the pan, add the capers and parsley and fry on a high heat for a few minutes (the capers might spit to begin with and the butter may become light golden brown, which is delicious). Spoon over the fish, then grate over the zest of half the lemon. Cut two wedges from the remaining lemon half and serve with the plaice.

Pork Loin Steaks with Apple & Sage

4 x 140g pork loin steaks
   (or 8 thinner steaks)
salt and freshly ground black pepper
small glug of olive oil
4–5 large sage leaves,
   roughly chopped
150ml apple juice or cider
1 tablespoon whole grain
   (seedy) mustard
5 tablespoons crème fraîche
a small handful of parsley leaves,
   roughly chopped, or fried sage
   leaves (see *Hints & Tips*)
   (optional)

These pork steaks are ready in no time at all, therefore are just the job for a last-minute supper. Delicious served with mashed or new potatoes or cooked pasta.

1. Dry the pork steaks on kitchen paper and snip through the fat of each one in two places, just through to the meat. This will stop it curling up during cooking. Season lightly with salt on both sides.

2. Heat the olive oil in a sauté pan, add the pork steaks and fry on a high heat for a few minutes until golden brown on the underside. Turn over, repeat and then transfer the steaks to a plate (you may need to do this in two batches to prevent overcrowding the pan, causing the steaks to stew and inhibit browning). If necessary, drain off all but ½ tablespoon of fat, leaving behind the tasty sediment.

3. On a low heat, add the sage and apple juice or cider to the pan and scrape the sediment off the bottom. Stir in the mustard and crème fraîche, bring up to a simmer, check the seasoning, then return the steaks and any juices to the pan. Simmer very gently for 5 minutes. Scatter with the parsley or fried sage leaves (if using) just before serving.

GET AHEAD

• Make this dish up to a day in advance, cool, cover and chill. Reheat gently in the sauté pan until hot and just beginning to bubble. You may need to loosen the sauce with a little water. Garnish with the parsley or fried sage leaves (if using) just before serving.

HINTS & TIPS

• If you have time, a few sage leaves fried in a little olive oil on a high heat for a minute or two until crisp, make a tasty garnish.

• Substitute chicken stock and ½ tablespoon of runny honey for the apple juice or cider.

• Savoy or sweetheart cabbage, very thinly shredded and steamed, boiled (only for 1 minute) or stir-fried until just wilted, is a perfect vegetable accompaniment.

• This dish can be frozen. Defrost before reheating gently in the sauté pan until hot and bubbling.

Bavette Steaks with Chimichurri Sauce

SERVES 2

2 bavette (flank) steaks,
   about 200g each
salt

For the chimichurri sauce
a small handful of parsley,
   including leaves and tender
   stems (about 10g)
2 plump garlic cloves, peeled
   (more if you like)
1 red (regular heat) chilli,
   de-seeded and finely chopped
½ teaspoon dried oregano
2 tablespoons red wine vinegar
8 tablespoons (120ml) olive oil
1 teaspoon salt
freshly ground black pepper,
   to taste

HINTS & TIPS

- For the chimichurri sauce, swap
  the fresh chilli for dried chilli flakes
  (add to taste) and 1–2 teaspoons
  of chopped fresh oregano for the
  dried.

- Chimichurri sauce is traditionally
  served with grilled, griddled or
  barbecued meat, fish and poultry
  in South America, where it's also
  used as a marinade. Any leftover
  sauce will keep (covered) in the
  fridge for several days. It's good
  on all sorts of things – you'll see!

This tasty cut of beef reminds me of the 'plat du jour' on a French menu, which is how I first enjoyed it years ago. Sometimes referred to as the 'butcher's cut', because butchers are said to keep it for themselves, it has a loose texture, a tasty, deep, rich flavour and it's inexpensive. Needing to be cooked quickly on a high heat to prevent it toughening, it's best served rare or medium-rare. The chimichurri sauce benefits from being made a few hours in advance, or even the day before, to give the flavours time to meld together.

I like to serve the steaks with Hasselback Potatoes (see page 144) and a leafy salad.

1. To make the chimichurri sauce, chop the parsley and garlic together quite finely yet still retaining a little texture. Put into a small bowl and stir in all the remaining ingredients. Taste and adjust any of the ingredients accordingly. Cover and set aside for a few hours, or chill overnight.

2. Put a dry griddle or frying pan on a high heat and rub the steaks all over with a little salt. When the pan is almost smoking hot, add the steaks. Cook on the high heat for 3 minutes, then turn over and cook for another 3 minutes. Transfer the steaks to a plate and keep somewhere warm for a minimum of 10 minutes (up to 30 minutes is fine, as long as they can be kept warm, not hot), to allow them to rest and reabsorb their juices.

3. Slice the steaks diagonally across the grain and serve with some chimichurri sauce spooned over the top, and the remainder separately.

Griddled Swordfish with Salsa Verde

SERVES 4

4 swordfish steaks (loins),
   each around 2.5cm thick,
   skin on or off
medium glug of olive oil
juice of ½ lemon
salt

For the salsa verde
6 anchovy fillets in oil, drained
1 tablespoon capers (in brine),
   drained
1 tablespoon cocktail gherkins,
   drained
1 garlic clove, peeled
2 large handfuls of parsley leaves
a handful of mint leaves (optional)
1 tablespoon fresh lemon juice
   (from the remaining
   ½ lemon above)
1 tablespoon Dijon mustard
8 tablespoons (120ml) olive oil
salt and freshly ground black pepper

Swordfish steaks are very tasty, succulent and juicy with a meaty texture, and are boneless to boot! Be careful not to overcook them though, as they quickly become dry and tough. As well as from fishmongers, they're available from many large supermarkets.

1. Put the swordfish steaks in a bowl, then pour over the olive oil and lemon juice to marinade.

2. Meanwhile, make the salsa verde. Blitz all the ingredients together using a stick blender, or in the small bowl of a food-processor (making sure not to over-process them into a paste), or finely chop them by hand. Check the seasoning and transfer to a bowl.

3. Heat a griddle pan for 5–10 minutes until very, very hot. Alternatively heat a frying pan, grill or barbecue.

4. Remove the swordfish steaks from the marinade, sprinkle with a little salt and then griddle on a high heat for 4 minutes until the flesh has turned white roughly halfway up the sides of the steaks (depending on the size of the griddle, you may need to do this in two batches). Turn the steaks over and cook for 2 minutes on the second side. They should be very juicy and barely cooked in the middle. Remove from the pan and rest for 5 minutes, before serving with the salsa verde.

GET AHEAD

• Make the salsa verde any time on
   the day. There will be some left over
   which will keep happily (covered)
   in the fridge for up to a week or so.

HINTS & TIPS

• Include other soft green herbs in the
   salsa verde (as well as the parsley
   and mint), such as tarragon, basil
   or chervil, if you have them to hand.

• Thinner swordfish steaks will take
   less time to cook.

• We love these with the Hasselback
   Potatoes (see page 144). New
   potatoes or mash are good, too,
   as are green vegetables or assorted
   salads.

Chicken, Mustard & Lemon Orzotto

SERVES 6

good glug or two of olive oil

4 medium-sized skinless, boneless
chicken thigh fillets, well-trimmed
and snipped into bite-sized (not
too small) chunks

salt and freshly ground black pepper

1 onion, finely chopped
(or use about 150g frozen
chopped onions)

300g dried orzo

3 teaspoons Dijon mustard

1 teaspoon English mustard

2 teaspoons black mustard seeds

750ml chicken stock
(or use 2 x 28g stock pots
or 2 stock cubes)

juice of 1 lemon

2 tablespoons double cream

3 tablespoons grated Parmesan
cheese (see tip on page 17),
plus (optional) extra for serving

a few handfuls of young or
baby spinach leaves (optional)

Creamy, luscious, fresh and sprightly aptly describe this tasty crowd-pleaser. The fact that it's inexpensive and a one-pan recipe as well just adds to its charm!

1. Heat the olive oil in a sauté pan or shallow casserole. Toss the chicken pieces in a little salt, add to the pan and cook on a high heat until light golden brown, then turn over and repeat (you may need to do this in a couple of batches so as not to overcrowd the pan). Transfer to a plate. The chicken won't be cooked through.

2. If necessary, add a little more olive oil to the pan, then add the onion and cook on a gentle heat for 10–15 minutes, until soft. Add the orzo, both mustards and the mustard seeds and stir until the orzo is coated. Add the stock (if using stock pots, add them in their concentrated form with 750ml of water, same for stock cubes, crumbling them in) and the chicken, bring to the boil and season. Reduce the heat and simmer very gently, uncovered, for 10 minutes, stirring occasionally. Stir in the lemon juice, cream and Parmesan. Check the seasoning. You may like to add a little water to loosen the mixture to your preferred consistency, making it as loose and creamy as you like.

3. Just before serving, add the spinach (if using) and stir until wilted. Serve, with a little bowl of extra Parmesan for sprinkling over the top, if you like.

GET AHEAD

- Complete to the end of step 2 up
to 2 days in advance. Cool, cover
and chill. To reheat, stir gently in
a pan on a moderate heat until
just bubbling and hot. It will almost
certainly need loosening with
some water.

HINTS & TIPS

- For a vegetarian orzotto, swap
the chicken for 400g of mushrooms
(any type, halved or sliced), use
vegetable stock, and swap the
Parmesan for a vegetarian Italian-
style hard cheese.

Courgette, Tomato & Mint Gnocchi

SERVES 4

salt and freshly ground black pepper
2 large or 4 smaller courgettes
(approx. 450g in total)
2 large ripe tomatoes
(approx. 250g in total)
4 tablespoons olive oil,
plus extra to serve
knob of butter
100ml vegetable (or chicken,
if not vegetarian) stock
(or use ½ stock cube)
2 mint sprigs, leaves picked
and stacked, rolled up and
very finely sliced into ribbons
1 x 500g packet chilled fresh
ready-made potato gnocchi
(400g packet is fine, too)

I am prone to describing some recipes as far greater than the sum of their ingredients, but this vegetarian recipe really is a perfect illustration of this. Juices from the courgettes and tomatoes meld beautifully with the stock, which are then emulsified with olive oil, transforming them into a delectable sauce, which in turn clings to the indentations in the gnocchi. Lovely summery ingredients brought alive with fresh mint – and if you have home-grown courgettes and tomatoes, that's a bonus!

1. Put a large pan of well-salted water on to boil for the gnocchi.

2. Meanwhile, cut the courgettes into quarters lengthways, then into 1cm-wide chunks. Quarter the tomatoes, cut into strips and then cut each strip into three chunks.

3. Heat 1 tablespoon of olive oil and the butter in a large frying pan, add the courgettes and cook on a high heat for about 5–8 minutes, turning from time to time, just until they begin to brown around the edges (depending on the size of the pan, you may need to do this in batches – if the pan is overcrowded, the courgettes will become soggy and won't brown).

4. Add the tomatoes, stock, most of the mint (reserving a little for garnishing) and some seasoning. Bring to the boil and then bubble rapidly for 3–4 minutes or so until the sauce has reduced a little, then add the remaining 3 tablespoons of olive oil. Shake the pan to emulsify the liquids together.

5. Meanwhile, cook the gnocchi in the pan of boiling water for a few minutes until it floats to the surface. Drain (or scoop out with a slotted spoon) and gently mix into the courgette sauce. Scatter over the reserved mint ribbons, finish with a swirl of olive oil and serve.

GET AHEAD

• Complete steps 2–4 any time on the day, cool, loosely cover and set aside at room temperature. Reheat gently in the pan until hot and bubbling before serving with the cooked gnocchi.

HINTS & TIPS

• Speed and a high heat are key to this recipe to avoid overcooked, soggy, stewed courgettes and tomatoes, which should both retain some shape/form and a little bit of bite.

• This courgette, tomato and mint sauce combo is also very good on cooked pasta.

Mushroom Stroganoff

SERVES 2

good glug of olive oil
1 shallot, finely sliced
300g mixed mushrooms, half thickly
   sliced, the remainder quartered
salt and freshly ground black pepper
1 garlic clove, crushed
½ teaspoon hot smoked paprika
1 teaspoon tomato purée
1 teaspoon Dijon mustard
150ml vegetable stock
   (or use ½ stock cube)
3 generous tablespoons soured
   cream or crème fraîche, plus
   a little extra to garnish
a small handful of parsley leaves,
   roughly chopped (optional)

This is a very quick, flavourful and inexpensive vegetarian main course. Be as adventurous as you like with the mushrooms. A few reliably-sourced wild mushrooms would be a lovely addition, too, if they're available. I like the little bit of heat from hot-smoked paprika, but use smoked or regular paprika, if you prefer. A pre-cooked pouch of rice for serving speeds things up even more if you're in a hurry.

1. Heat the olive oil in a medium-sized frying or sauté pan, add the shallot and cook on a gentle heat for 5 minutes, or until soft. Add the mushrooms and some seasoning and fry on a high heat, stirring, until cooked, any moisture has evaporated and they begin to sizzle.

2. Add the garlic and hot smoked paprika and cook for another minute before adding the tomato purée, mustard and stock. Bring to the boil, check the seasoning and simmer rapidly until reduced by about half and thickened a little into a sauce, around 5 minutes.

3. Add the soured cream or crème fraîche and stir over the heat just until it comes up to the boil. Check the seasoning: it should be very flavourful. Serve from the pan, or transfer to a serving dish or platter, and garnish with a few dots or diagonal stripes of soured cream or crème fraîche, interspersed with chopped parsley. Serve with cooked rice, either plain or pre-mixed Basmati and wild rice.

GET AHEAD

- The whole recipe can be completed up to 3 days in advance, cooled, covered and chilled (but don't garnish until just before serving). Reheat gently in a pan until hot and bubbling.

HINTS & TIPS

- Cooking the rice at the same time as the stroganoff ensures that everything will be ready together (unless you're using a ready-cooked pouch of rice that just needs heating through).

- Chicken stock can be used if a vegetarian dish isn't essential.

- A shake or two of mushroom ketchup can be added for extra flavour, if you have it.

Chicken Satay

SERVES 4

vegetable oil, for cooking
500g skinless, boneless chicken
   thigh fillets, breasts or breast
   fillets/tenders, cut into bite-sized
   chunks or strips
2 tablespoons Thai red curry paste
   (see *Hints & Tips*)
3 tablespoons peanut butter
   (ideally smooth, but any will do)
1 teaspoon demerara sugar
1 teaspoon dark soy sauce
2 teaspoons fish sauce
1 x 400g tin coconut milk
juice of ½ lime

To garnish (optional)
1 tablespoon roasted or plain
   peanuts (more if you like),
   roughly chopped; dried chilli
   flakes; roughly chopped parsley;
   2 spring onions, trimmed
   and sliced diagonally, if you
   have them

A no-frills supper, but exceedingly tasty nonetheless, this dish is pretty much made with store cupboard ingredients. If you use a pouch of cooked jasmine rice, which is also a great store cupboard standby, it becomes super-speedy. Just pick up some chicken and you're off and running…

1. Heat a splash of vegetable oil in a (preferably non-stick) wok or sauté pan. Add some of the chicken (being careful not to overcrowd the pan, otherwise it will stew rather than fry) and stir-fry on a high heat for a few minutes until beginning to brown and it's just cooked through. Transfer to a plate and repeat with the remaining chicken, adding a little more oil if necessary.

2. Heat another splash of vegetable oil in the pan, add the Thai red curry paste and stir-fry over a medium heat for a minute, then add the peanut butter, sugar, and soy and fish sauces. Mix together, then add the coconut milk and lime juice and simmer gently for a few minutes. Check the seasoning and add a little more soy or fish sauce if needed and thin with a little water if necessary.

3. Return the chicken to the pan and simmer for a few minutes until warmed through, giving it the odd stir. If you prefer a thinner consistency, thin with a little water. Top with any or all of the garnishes (if using) and serve.

GET AHEAD

- The recipe can be made up to 3 days in advance. Cool, cover and chill. Reheat in a pan on a low heat until hot and bubbling. Loosen with a little water, if necessary.

HINTS & TIPS

- 'Thai Red Curry Paste Shots' from M&S come in packs of four individual pots, which rather handily contain exactly 2 tablespoons each. Otherwise it's available in jars.

- Serve with cooked rice (jasmine is particularly good) or flat rice noodles, and a lightly cooked green vegetable such as pak choi, French beans or spinach, if you like.

- Swap the chicken for pork tenderloin (fillet), cut into finger-sized strips.

Peppered Tuna Steaks with Tomato, Lemon & Herb Sauce

SERVES 2

salt
2 x 140–150g tuna steaks,
   each about 2–2.5cm thick
   (ideally the latter)
½ tablespoon cracked or coarsely
   ground black pepper
olive oil, for cooking
100g baby plum tomatoes, halved
   (choose mixed colours, if you like)
a good handful of fresh herbs,
   such as basil, parsley, tarragon,
   mint, oregano and chives (any of,
   or a mixture of), roughly chopped
juice of ½ lemon

HINTS & TIPS

• Swap cherry tomatoes for the baby
  plum tomatoes, if you prefer.

Speedy, speedy, speedy! When eating this, my husband John always wonders how something that's so quick to make (10 minutes max) can be so delicious. You'll have to try it to find out! Tuna steaks only take a minute to cook on each side and I would advise sticking to this, however short a time that might seem to you. We love this with the Cauliflower Purée (see page 159).

1. Rub a little salt into the tuna steaks and lightly sprinkle both sides with the black pepper, pressing down to help it stick. Smear the steaks on both sides with a little olive oil. Heat a dry frying pan until smoking hot, then add the tuna steaks and cook on a high heat for exactly 1 minute on each side (if the steaks are less than 2cm thick, cook for 45 seconds only on both sides). Transfer to a plate and keep warm. Wipe out the pan.

2. Heat a generous glug of olive oil in the same frying pan, add the tomatoes and some salt and cook on a medium heat for a minute or two, until softened and beginning to collapse, but still just holding their shape. Stir in the herbs and lemon juice, add a little more olive oil if necessary, and shake the pan to form an emulsified sauce. Check the seasoning.

3. Cut the tuna steaks in half diagonally and on a slant, and prop up against each other on each plate, forming a criss-cross and spoon over the tomato sauce and serve.

One-pan Spicy Sausages & Beans

SERVES 4

olive oil, for cooking
8 sausages of your choice
 (I like fat Italian-style ones)
1 onion, finely chopped
 (or use about 150g frozen
 chopped onions)
1 teaspoon rose harissa paste
1 teaspoon Dijon mustard
good pinch of dried oregano
good pinch of granulated sugar
1 x 28g chicken stock pot
1 x 400g tin plum or
 chopped tomatoes
2 x 400g tins haricot beans,
 drained and rinsed
salt and freshly ground black pepper
120g young or baby spinach leaves
 (optional)

Sausage and beans by any other name, but so much nicer thanks to gentle spicing and heat from the harissa paste and a few other additions. A lovely, warming supper that is on the table in about 30 minutes. I sometimes ring the changes by putting a slice of toasted sourdough in the bottom of individual bowls and spooning the sausage casserole over the top – hey presto, sausages and beans on toast!

1. Heat a splash of olive oil in a sauté pan, add the sausages and cook on a medium-high heat until browned all over. Transfer to a plate.

2. Add a little more oil to the pan if necessary, add the onion and cook on a low heat for around 10 minutes until soft. Add the harissa paste, mustard, oregano, sugar, stock pot, tomatoes and haricot beans. Rinse the tomato tin out with a little water (about a quarter of a tinful) and add this to the pan, along with some seasoning. Return the sausages to the pan, bring up to a simmer, check the seasoning, then bubble gently for 15 minutes, adding a little more water if necessary.

3. Just before serving, add the spinach (if using), a handful at a time, allowing it to semi-wilt between each addition. Serve.

GET AHEAD

• Steps 1 and 2 can be completed any time on the day and left at room temperature. Or make up to 3 days in advance, cool, cover and chill. It can also be frozen (defrost before reheating). For all options, reheat gently in a pan until hot and bubbling, giving it the odd stir. You'll need to add a little more water to loosen the mixture.

HINTS & TIPS

• The better the quality of the sausages, the more delicious this will be.

• Although filling, if you're feeding a hungry tribe, you may like to add one or two more sausages and/or serve with mashed or baked potatoes or soft polenta.

Duck Breasts with Cannellini Bean Ragout & Plum Sauce

SERVES 2

2 duck breasts, trimmed, the skin
  scored in a criss-cross pattern
salt and freshly ground black pepper
4 spring onions, trimmed
  and thinly sliced diagonally
1 large garlic clove, crushed
120g young, baby or regular spinach
3 tablespoons crème fraîche
  (more if you like)
1 x 400g tin cannellini beans,
  drained and rinsed

For the plum sauce
1 tablespoon good-quality plum jam
¼ x 28g chicken stock pot
  (see *Hints & Tips*)
good grinding of black pepper

GET AHEAD

• As long as they're kept warm, the
  duck breasts will rest happily for
  an hour or so. The ragout can then
  be made to the end of step 3 and
  set aside in the pan until required,
  leaving very little to do at the last
  minute.

HINTS & TIPS

• Substitute apricot jam in the
  absence of plum jam.

• Save the remaining stock pot
  for another dish.

This is a speedy and very tasty supper, which can easily be doubled. Just use a slightly larger frying pan. The ridiculously easy plum sauce is very good with duck legs, too, and lasts for weeks in the fridge.

1. Put the plum sauce ingredients into a small pan, stir in 6 tablespoons (90ml) of water, bring to the boil and cook on a high heat for a few minutes until reduced to a sauce. Set aside.

2. Heat a small or medium dry frying pan on a high heat, sprinkle the skin of the duck breasts with a little salt and add them to the pan, skin-side down. Reduce the heat to medium and cook for 5 minutes, until brown and crisp. Turn the breasts over, reduce the heat to low and cook for another 5 minutes. Transfer to a plate and keep warm.

3. Discard all but 1 tablespoon of fat from the pan (discard it all if it's burnt, wipe the pan out with kitchen paper and add 1 tablespoon of olive oil), add the spring onions and cook on a low-medium heat for a few minutes, stirring, until beginning to soften. Add the garlic, cook for a further minute, then add the spinach, a splash of water and some seasoning and cook just until the spinach begins to collapse but is still holding its shape.

4. Stir in the crème fraîche, bubble it up, then add the cannellini beans and simmer the ragout on a low heat for a minute or two until it's thickened a little, but still 'saucy'. Check the seasoning. Reheat the plum sauce.

5. Slice the duck breasts (stir any juices from the plate into the ragout). Divide the ragout between two plates, arrange the duck breasts on top, spoon over the plum sauce and serve.

Bowl Food from Around the World

This chapter comes with the caveat that I am using the term 'around the world' loosely. I wouldn't presume to suggest these recipes are authentic or anything like, but simply my interpretation of some of the flavours and food from other countries traditionally served in bowls. Some are best served in deep bowls and others in wide shallow ones, showing off the different ingredients. One thing's for sure though, they're all very flavourful!

One-pan Hake with Peppers & Chickpeas

SERVES 4

generous glug of olive oil,
  plus extra for drizzling
1 large onion, thinly sliced
  (or you could use 200g frozen
  chopped onions)
1 red pepper, halved, de-seeded
  and thinly sliced lengthways
salt and freshly ground black pepper
2 garlic cloves, sliced
500g ripe tomatoes, quartered,
  then cut into chunks
1 teaspoon paprika
1 tablespoon tomato purée
200ml white wine
150ml fish, vegetable or chicken
  stock (or use 1 stock cube)
1 x 400g tin chickpeas, drained
  and rinsed
4 hake fillets, about 150–160g
  each, skinned and seasoned
a small handful of coriander,
  roughly chopped

A tenuous version of Cataplana, the traditional Portuguese dish, which I learnt from a chef in Portugal, but made quicker here by swapping the customary potatoes (which take longer to cook) for chickpeas, as I sometimes do for a speedier supper. It doesn't take away from the gorgeous traditional Cataplana flavours, although I expect a chef would favour the potato version!

1. Heat the olive oil in a lidded sauté pan. Add the onion, red pepper and a little salt and cook on a medium heat for 5 minutes, giving it the odd stir. Add the garlic, tomatoes, paprika, tomato purée and some seasoning and cook for a further 5 minutes, stirring from time to time. Add the wine and stock and bring to the boil. Check the seasoning, then simmer gently for 15 minutes, stirring occasionally. Stir in the chickpeas.

2. Bring back up to a simmer, place the seasoned hake fillets on top, drizzle with some more olive oil, cover with the lid and simmer gently for 5–7 minutes until the hake is just cooked through. The exact time will depend on the thickness of the fillets.

3. Serve spooned into shallow bowls, scattered with the coriander. A green salad and some crusty bread for mopping up would be good accompaniments.

GET AHEAD

• Step 1 can be completed up to 3 days in advance, cooled, covered and chilled. The sauce can also be frozen (defrost before reheating). For both options, reheat gently in the pan until hot and bubbling before adding the fish as above.

HINTS & TIPS

• Loosen the sauce with a little water if necessary.

• This is a handy recipe for entertaining as it's mostly made in advance, with the fish taking only a few minutes to cook just before eating.

• This also works well with most other white fish fillets.

Bacon, Blue Cheese & Spinach Gnocchi

SERVES 3–4

2 tablespoons olive oil
1 x 500g packet chilled fresh
  ready-made potato gnocchi
  (400g packet is fine, too)
6 rashers smoked streaky bacon,
  stacked up and snipped into
  roughly 1cm batons
120g creamy blue cheese,
  such as Saint Agur, Gorgonzola
  or Dolcelatte
3 heaped tablespoons crème fraîche
120g baby spinach leaves
salt and freshly ground black pepper
2 large spring onions, trimmed
  and finely chopped (optional)
a small handful of walnut pieces,
  toasted and roughly chopped
  (optional) (see *Hints & Tips*)

HINTS & TIPS

• To toast walnuts, put a handful of
  walnut pieces (or halves) into a
  small, dry frying pan and cook on
  a medium heat for a few minutes,
  while stirring, until fragrant and
  lightly browned. Leave to cool, then
  chop.

• This is very good served with a bitter
  leaf salad, such as radicchio or
  chicory, or crisp salad leaves with
  peppery watercress and rocket
  leaves. A few walnuts would also
  be a nice addition to the salad, as
  would a little walnut oil in the salad
  dressing.

A lovely comforting bowl of creamy gnocchi, spiked with bacon and blue cheese. The gnocchi are fried, therefore everything's cooked in one pan – it really couldn't be much simpler.

1. Heat the olive oil in a large, non-stick frying pan, add the gnocchi and fry on a high heat until beginning to turn golden brown. Allow them to form a crust on the bottom before turning over with a fish slice, then turn from time to time until golden brown all over, about 5–10 minutes in all. Transfer to a plate.

2. Add the bacon to the now dry pan and fry on a high heat until turning golden brown and sizzling. Lower the heat, crumble the cheese into the pan, add the crème fraîche and heat gently, stirring to make a smooth, creamy sauce. Add the spinach, a handful at a time, and stir until partially wilted between each addition. Season with black pepper, and salt if it needs it.

3. Return the gnocchi to the pan and heat through, very gently stirring everything together over the low heat. Add a little more crème fraîche or a splash of water if you prefer a creamier consistency. Serve in individual bowls scattered with the spring onions and toasted walnuts (if using) and finish with a grinding of black pepper.

Bulhao Pato (Portuguese Clams)

SERVES 4

1kg fresh live clams (in their shells)
1 teaspoon salt, plus extra
 for seasoning
4 tablespoons olive oil
4 plump garlic cloves, chopped
250ml white wine
juice of 1 lemon
around 20g coriander (thick stems
 discarded), roughly chopped
freshly ground black pepper

GET AHEAD

• Step 2 can be completed any time
 on the day and left in the pan, ready
 to make the recipe in no time at all
 when required.

HINTS & TIPS

• For a change, try adding some
 chorizo to the clams. In the dry
 saucepan, cook a 12–15cm piece
 of spicy (salami-style) chorizo
 (peeled, halved and cut into ½cm-
 thick half-moon slices) on a medium
 heat for 1–2 minutes, until the fat
 begins to run, before continuing
 with step 2.

Fresh, light, ridiculously easy and so quick! We love this classic Portuguese recipe as a light lunch after the fish van has called. You'll need some good artisan bread for mopping up.

1. Soak the clams in a bowl of cold water with the measured salt for an hour or so. Tap any open shells and if they don't shut, discard along with any damaged shells, then drain and rinse.

2. Gently heat the olive oil in a lidded saucepan, add the garlic and cook on a low heat for a few minutes, stirring, until fragrant and just beginning to turn a pale biscuit colour.

3. Add the clams and the white wine, cover with the lid and shake the pan on a high heat for 3 minutes until the clams have just opened. Remove from the heat and discard any shells that haven't opened. Stir in the lemon juice and coriander. Check and adjust the seasoning. Divide between four bowls and serve with some good artisan bread.

Tomato & Coconut Dhal

SERVES 4

For the dhal
250g dried red split lentils
1 onion, thinly sliced (or use
  around 150g frozen chopped
  onions)
1 teaspoon ground turmeric
1½ teaspoons medium curry powder
¼ teaspoon ground cinnamon
⅛ teaspoon medium chilli powder
a small handful of dried curry
  leaves, roughly crushed
1 x 28g vegetable stock pot
  or 1 vegetable stock cube
1 x 400g tin coconut milk
400g tomatoes, half of one reserved
  for garnish, the remainder
  chunkily chopped
salt and freshly ground black pepper

To serve (optional)
soft-boiled eggs (lowered into
  boiling water for 6½ minutes,
  then into cold water and peeled
  when just cool enough to handle);
  nigella or onion seeds; roughly
  chopped coriander; natural
  yoghurt (dairy-free, such as
  coconut yoghurt, for a vegan dhal)

This is pretty much a store cupboard recipe, at least it is for me. Gently spiced, it has warmth without fire, is creamy from the coconut milk, and immensely satisfying. It's good to also know that as long as I've got some tomatoes, I'm minutes away from a quick lunch, particularly in mid-winter when it's blowing a hooley outside. All the ingredients, except the tomatoes, go into the pan together at the outset, so it's nice and simple, too. Suitable for vegetarians, and for vegans as well, if you omit the optional eggs.

1. Put all the dhal ingredients, except the tomatoes and salt and pepper into a large pan. Fill the empty coconut milk tin with water and add that, then bring the mixture to the boil, stirring from time to time. Simmer on a low heat, stirring occasionally, for 10 minutes.

2. Add the tomatoes and simmer gently for a further 15 minutes, stirring occasionally. If necessary, thin with a little more water to your preferred consistency (bearing in mind the dhal will thicken up if not eating it immediately). Season with salt and pepper.

3. Divide the dhal between four bowls, thinly slice the reserved tomato and arrange on top with any, or all, of the serving suggestions (if using), and serve.

GET AHEAD

• The recipe can be completed to
the end of step 2 up to 3 days in
advance, then cooled, covered
and chilled, or it can be frozen
(defrost before reheating). For
both options, reheat gently in
a pan until hot and bubbling.

HINTS & TIPS

• This is a lovely dhal without the
tomatoes. Add a few handfuls of
spinach (young or regular leaves)
at the end if you like (just allow it
to wilt), with or without the tomatoes.

Singapore Noodles

SERVES 2

2 x 50g/55g nests dried thin
  vermicelli rice noodles,
  or 300g fresh rice noodles
sesame oil, for drizzling and cooking
2 teaspoons medium curry powder
¼ teaspoon ground turmeric
1 teaspoon granulated sugar
2 tablespoons dry sherry
3 tablespoons dark soy sauce
bunch of spring onions, trimmed
  and chunkily sliced diagonally
12 raw peeled king or tiger prawns
2 garlic cloves, crushed
1 teaspoon ginger purée from
  a jar or tube
1 mild red chilli, de-seeded
  and finely chopped
2 eggs, lightly beaten
110g frozen peas
freshly chopped coriander and
  lime wedges, to serve (optional)

As with most stir fries, it's important, and much easier, to prepare all the components before you start cooking. As this is a very quick way of cooking, they're then ready at hand to add in quick succession to the wok. After that it takes a matter of just a few minutes to cook. Assuming you have noodles in the cupboard, you're only a few minutes away from a tasty quick lunch or supper. Using fresh noodles is quicker still.

1. If using dried noodles, soak or cook them according to the packet instructions. Drain and toss with a splash of sesame oil to prevent sticking, then set aside. Fresh noodles need no preparation.

2. Mix the curry powder, turmeric, sugar, sherry and soy sauce together in a small bowl.

3. Heat a good splash of sesame oil in a (preferably non-stick) wok on a high heat until very hot, then add the spring onions, prawns, garlic, ginger and chilli and stir-fry for 1–2 minutes or just until the prawns turn pink. Lower the heat. Push everything to one side of the wok, then tilt it, add a drop more sesame oil, and pour in the beaten eggs in a thin layer. Cook as for a thin omelette, until set, then break up into ribbons and combine with the other wok ingredients.

4. Stir in the peas and noodles, warm through, then add the soy sauce mixture. Mix well and cook on a low-medium heat until hot throughout. Add a little water if the noodles seem dry. Serve immediately garnished with chopped coriander and lime wedges (if using).

GET AHEAD

- Step 2 can be completed up to
  2 days in advance and kept in a
  covered bowl at room temperature.

HINTS & TIPS

- Substitute a good pinch of dried
  chilli flakes for the fresh chilli,
  a thinly sliced shallot for the
  spring onions, and parsley for
  the coriander.

- Add any cooked vegetables you
  have to hand, with, or instead of,
  the peas.

- Thin slices of pork tenderloin (fillet)
  or cooked pork (or raw or cooked
  chicken) can be added with the
  prawns, as can some thinly sliced
  mushrooms, such as shiitake.
  A handful or two of beansprouts
  can be added with the noodles.

- In step 4, you may find it easier to
  combine everything by snipping the
  odd clump or two of noodles with
  scissors, to shorten their length.

Pearl Barley Ratatouille 'Risotto'

SERVES 4

good glug of olive oil,
  plus extra to serve
1 onion, finely chopped
  (or use about 150g frozen
  chopped onions)
1 medium aubergine, sliced
  lengthways and cut into
  roughly 1cm dice
salt and freshly ground black pepper
2 garlic cloves, crushed
½ teaspoon dried oregano
1 red pepper, halved, de-seeded
  and cut into roughly 1cm dice
150g pearl barley
1 x 400g tin chopped
  or plum tomatoes
400ml vegetable stock
  (or use chicken, if not vegetarian),
  or use 1 stock cube
1 medium courgette, cut into
  roughly 1cm dice
12 pitted black olives, halved
4 knobs of butter

To serve (optional)
basil leaves
a small bowl of grated vegetarian
  (or vegan) Italian-style hard cheese

A pearl barley 'risotto' studded with Mediterranean vegetables, this makes an unfussy, healthy and speedy vegetarian supper. It is deeply flavourful with a lovely, nutty, chewy bite from the pearl barley. If you omit the butter, it's also vegan (a dollop of coconut yoghurt would be a perfect vegan alternative).

1. Heat the olive oil in a lidded sauté pan (around 24 x 6cm), add the onion, aubergine and some seasoning and cook on a low heat for 10 minutes, stirring occasionally, until softened. Add a little more olive oil if necessary as they cook, but the aubergine will soak up as much as you give it, so don't be tempted to add too much. Add the garlic, oregano, red pepper and pearl barley and stir over the heat for a minute or two.

2. Add the tomatoes and stock, or, if using a cube, fill the empty tomato tin with water, add it to the pan and crumble over the stock cube. Bring to the boil, while stirring, then add generous seasoning. Cover and simmer very gently for 30 minutes, giving it the odd stir and adding a little more water if all the liquid has been absorbed.

3. Stir in the courgette and black olives, bring back to a simmer, and simmer, uncovered, for a further 10 minutes, until the barley is plumped and tender but still chewy and the courgette retains a little bite. You may need to loosen the mixture with a little water – it should be just on the sloppy side, rather than dry or runny. Check the seasoning.

4. Serve in bowls with a knob of butter nestled into the middle of each serving, a scattering of basil leaves (if using) and an extra swirl of olive oil. Hand around the cheese separately (if using).

GET AHEAD

• Step 1 can be completed up to a day in advance. Cool, cover and chill. Reheat gently in the pan until hot throughout, then continue as above.

HINTS & TIPS

• This recipe is nothing if it's not well seasoned, so do keep checking!

Tiger Prawns in Spicy Coconut Sauce

SERVES 4

good glug of vegetable oil
1 onion, finely chopped
   (or use about 150g frozen
   chopped onions)
1 garlic clove, crushed
1 teaspoon ground turmeric
1 teaspoon medium curry powder
1 teaspoon ginger purée
   from a jar or tube
1 red or green chilli (regular heat),
   de-seeded and finely chopped
½ teaspoon ground cinnamon
½ fish (or vegetable or chicken)
   stock cube
½ teaspoon salt
freshly ground black pepper
1 x 400g tin coconut milk
1 lime, ½ juiced, ½ cut into
   4 wedges
3 tablespoons double cream
1 tomato, roughly chopped
220g Basmati rice, or 4 x 50g/55g
   nests dried egg or rice noodles
450g (frozen weight) raw peeled
   tiger prawns, defrosted
   and rinsed

A really quick supper that can almost be entirely cooked in advance, leaving a 2-minute task just before eating. Gently spiced, the recipe uses mainly store cupboard ingredients. Try to buy the largest, plumpest raw prawns you can, with or without their tail shells. The tail shells look good but are more fiddly to eat, unless that is, you like eating the shells!

1. Heat the vegetable oil in a sauté pan and cook the onion on a low heat until softened, about 10 minutes.

2. Add the garlic, turmeric, curry powder, ginger, chilli, cinnamon, stock cube, salt and a generous grinding of black pepper and continue to cook on a low heat for 3–4 minutes, while stirring.

3. Add the coconut milk to the pan, bring to the boil, stirring occasionally, then simmer gently for 10 minutes. Check the seasoning – it will probably need more salt. Stir in the lime juice, double cream and the chopped tomato.

4. While the sauce is simmering, cook the rice or noodles according to the packet instructions.

5. Add the prawns to the sauce and cook gently for a minute or two, just until they turn pink. Divide the cooked rice or noodles between four bowls. Spoon over the prawn mixture and serve immediately with the lime wedges. A lightly cooked green vegetable, such as pak choi or spinach, is a perfect accompaniment.

GET AHEAD

• The recipe can be completed to the end of step 3 up to 3 days in advance, cooled, covered and chilled. If using on the day, cool, cover loosely and leave at room temperature. It can also be frozen (defrost before reheating). For all options, reheat gently in the pan until hot and bubbling before adding the prawns as above.

HINTS & TIPS

• The prawns can be replaced, or added to, with chunks of raw monkfish or other white fish, or with bite-sized pieces of raw chicken meat. These will take a few minutes longer than the prawns to cook.

• If you're in a hurry, pouches of ready-cooked rice or noodles save time.

Pappardelle with Sausagemeat & Fennel Ragù

SERVES 4

good glug of olive oil
1 onion, finely chopped
  (or use about 150g frozen
  chopped onions)
1 medium or 2 small fennel
  bulbs, tough outer layer and stems
  discarded (but fronds reserved),
  halved and thinly sliced
salt and freshly ground black pepper
200g sausagemeat (flavour
  of your choice)
½ teaspoon dried oregano
2 garlic cloves, crushed
250g cherry tomatoes, halved
500g fresh pappardelle

To serve and garnish
grated Parmesan cheese
  (see tip on page 17)
a few basil leaves (optional)
reserved fennel fronds (optional)

This recipe came about after having some sausagemeat leftover at Christmas, and some fennel lurking, too. As the two make great bedfellows, this seemed the obvious thing to make. I've suggested using fresh pappardelle for speediness, as it only takes 4 minutes to cook, but by all means use dried pasta if you prefer, in which case you will need less (about 400g).

1. Heat the olive oil in a sauté pan or shallow casserole, large enough to accommodate the pasta later on. Add the onion, fennel and a pinch of salt and cook on a low heat until soft, but not coloured, stirring occasionally, about 10 minutes.

2. Increase the heat to medium-high, add the sausagemeat and fry, stirring and breaking it up into different 'rubble'-sized pieces, until beginning to brown, about 5 minutes. Don't worry if it sticks to the pan a little, it will be released when the tomatoes are added.

3. Add the oregano, garlic, tomatoes and some seasoning and cook on a low-medium heat for a further 5 minutes, giving it the odd stir, until the tomatoes have partly collapsed and the mixture has melded into a delicious (slightly chunky) sauce. Check the seasoning.

4. Meanwhile, bring a large pan of well-salted water to the boil and cook the pasta according to the packet instructions. Scoop out and reserve a mugful of the water, then drain the pasta. Add it to the sauce in the pan and then toss the two together, adding a little of the reserved pasta water to loosen it, if you like.

5. Divide between four (wide, rather than deep) bowls, sprinkle with a little Parmesan cheese, garnish with the roughly chopped fennel fronds and a few basil leaves (if using), and serve.

GET AHEAD

• Complete to the end of step 3 up to 3 days in advance, cool, cover and chill. It can also be frozen (defrost before reheating). For both options, reheat gently in a pan until hot and bubbling, then continue as above.

HINTS & TIPS

• The better quality the sausagemeat you use, the better this will taste. Alternatively, use your favourite sausages and slit and discard their skins.

• Add a splash or two of double cream to the ragù at the end of step 3 for a creamy sauce.

Chicken Ramen

1 litre chicken stock
2 garlic cloves, thinly sliced
1 teaspoon ginger purée
    from a jar or tube
3–4 tablespoons dark soy sauce
    (depending on the strength
    of the stock)
dried chilli flakes, to taste
4 x 50g/55g nests dried egg
    or rice noodles
4 handfuls of baby spinach leaves
around 400g cooked chicken
    meat, shredded
2 spring onions, trimmed and
    thinly sliced diagonally
mixed black and white sesame
    seeds, toasted (see *Hints & Tips*
    on page 40), for sprinkling
4 soft-boiled eggs (cooked for
    6½ minutes in boiling water,
    cooled in cold water), peeled
    and halved

Your ramen, or Japanese noodle soup, will be as good as the stock you use. It goes without saying that home-made stock is best, but as this is a quicker, shortcut version of ramen, the best quality ready-made stock you can find will be fine. There are some very good stocks available, either fresh, or in pouches with a long shelf life. I usually make ramen when I've got leftover cooked meat or poultry to use up, but it's well worth buying steak or chicken thigh fillets and cooking them especially, too. A very satisfying, inexpensive bowl of goodness and warmth.

1. Put the stock into a saucepan with the garlic, ginger, 3 tablespoons of soy sauce and a small pinch of chilli flakes, then bring to the boil and simmer gently for 5 minutes. Check the seasoning and adjust if need be – you may like to add more soy and/or chilli flakes.

2. Cook the noodles according to the packet instructions, then drain and divide between four warmed bowls, followed by a handful of spinach leaves in each. Bring the broth back up to the boil and then ladle into the bowls over the spinach. Top with the chicken, scatter over the spring onions and some toasted sesame seeds and arrange the egg halves to one side of each bowl. Serve immediately – with napkins!

HINTS & TIPS

- Cooked vegetables such as pak choi, tenderstem broccoli, shredded kale and chard can be added to the ramen, as can beansprouts.

- Substitute the chicken for cooked pork, beef or lamb. Alternatively, snip 4 raw skinless, boneless chicken thigh fillets into strips and cook in the simmering broth for 3–4 minutes. Remove from the broth with a slotted spoon and divide between the bowls. Or, cook 1–2 beef steaks rare, slice thinly and divide between the bowls in place of the chicken.

- For vegetarians, in place of the chicken stock and chicken, use vegetable stock and 400g of mushrooms (any type), sliced and fried in a splash of vegetable oil with salt and pepper, or use a handful or two of cooked leftover green veggies.

- Use sachets of 'straight-to-wok noodles' (or similar), if you prefer. If using chilled fresh noodles, you'll need about 550g for the four servings.

Bibimbap

1 x 225–250g steak (I like rib-eye)
dark soy sauce, for coating
125g raw Basmati rice or 1 x 250g
   ready-cooked pouch Basmati rice
salt and freshly ground black pepper
sesame oil, for coating and cooking
150g shiitake (or other) mushrooms,
   thinly sliced
1 carrot, peeled and shredded
   into thin strips with a mandolin
   or by hand, or grated
150g young or regular spinach leaves
2 eggs
2 spring onions, trimmed and
   thinly sliced diagonally
mixed black and white sesame seeds

For the pickled cucumber
¼ cucumber, thinly sliced
   (I use a mandolin)
¼ teaspoon salt
1 teaspoon granulated sugar
1 teaspoon toasted sesame oil
1 tablespoon white wine vinegar

For the sauce
2 tablespoons gochujang paste
½ tablespoon sesame oil
1 teaspoon dark soy sauce
1 teaspoon granulated sugar
1 teaspoon white sesame seeds,
   toasted (see *Hints & Tips* on
   page 40)

Probably the most well-known of Korean dishes, Bibimbap is quite simply delicious. I certainly don't claim this adaptation to be authentic; however, as the essence of the recipe is a rice bowl topped with meat, a fried egg, and/or vegetables, it conforms to that, and of course, includes gochujang, the vital ingredient that brings all the other components together. Gochujang is a hot, sweet, spicy and slightly addictive chilli paste and is available from Asian supermarkets, most large supermarkets and online.

1. Mix the pickled cucumber ingredients together in a small bowl. Set aside. Mix the sauce ingredients together in a separate bowl, adding ½ tablespoon of water. Set aside. Rub the steak all over with a little soy sauce and set aside.

2. Cook the raw rice with ½ teaspoon of salt according to the packet instructions, or heat the pouch of rice according to the packet instructions. Divide between two bowls and keep warm.

3. Meanwhile, heat a small, dry frying pan. Rub a little sesame oil over the steak and cook in the pan on a high heat for 2–3 minutes on each side (or until cooked to your liking). Transfer to a plate and leave to rest somewhere warm.

4. Add the mushrooms and some seasoning to the pan and fry on a high heat in the residual fat from the steak (add a splash of sesame oil if the fat is scarce) until beginning to brown. Divide the mushrooms between each bowl, spooned into a clump on top of the rice.

5. Add a small splash of sesame oil to the pan and fry the carrot strips with a little salt on a high heat, just until they begin to wilt, about 1 minute. Add to the rice bowls in another clump.

6. Add the spinach to the pan with a pinch of salt and a splash of water and cook on a high heat for a minute, until wilted. Drain, squeeze out the excess liquid with the back of a spoon and add to the rice bowls in another clump.

7. Lift the pickled cucumber out of its liquid with a spoon, leaving the liquid behind, and add to the rice bowls as before, then spoon over a little of the liquid (discard the remainder).

8. Slice the steak on an angle and divide between the bowls in a final clump. Divide any beef juices between the bowls.

9. Lastly, fry the two eggs in a little sesame oil (the yolks should be runny), then transfer one to each bowl, followed by a small dollop of the sauce to the side. Scatter with the spring onions and a few mixed sesame seeds, and serve. Traditionally, the runny egg yolk is broken and mixed with the sauce, which in turn is mixed into everything else. Serve the remaining sauce separately.

GET AHEAD

• The mushrooms, carrot and spring onions can be prepared the day before and kept chilled. The sauce can be made up to 3 days in advance, and the cucumber can be completed any time on the day. Keep both covered at room temperature. The steak can be rubbed with soy sauce any time on the day and also kept covered at room temperature.

HINTS & TIPS

• Any leftover sauce will keep (covered) in the fridge for a week or more. Try drizzling it over eggs (cooked in any way), or in sauces, stews, soups, dipping sauces, mayonnaise and dressings.

• Once opened, a jar or tub of gochujang paste will last for several weeks in the fridge or it can be frozen.

• For vegetarians, you could replace the steak with the same weight of diced firm tofu (soy-coated as for the steak), fried in a little sesame oil on a medium heat for 1–2 minutes, turning regularly, until golden all over, and/or some beansprouts, raw courgette and/or radish matchsticks, or just increase the vegetable quantities in the main recipe.

Salmon Poke Bowl

SERVES 2

150g sushi (sticky) or jasmine rice,
  rinsed under cold water in a sieve
  until the water runs clear
1 tablespoon rice/rice wine vinegar
75g frozen (podded) edamame beans
salt
150g very fresh salmon fillet,
  skinned and cut into 1.5cm cubes
1 small carrot, peeled and
  shredded or grated
Pickled Cucumber (see page 112),
  or pickled red cabbage, red onion
  or ginger, or other pickles
  from a jar
1 ripe avocado, halved, stoned and
  thinly sliced within its skin
2 spring onions, trimmed and
  thinly sliced diagonally
mixed black and white sesame
  seeds, toasted (see *Hints & Tips*
  on page 40)

For the marinade
1 tablespoon dark soy sauce
½ tablespoon rice/rice wine vinegar
½ tablespoon toasted sesame oil
small pinch of dried chilli flakes

For the sauce
2 tablespoons thick mayonnaise
  (see notes on page 17)
½ teaspoon dark soy sauce
¼ teaspoon sesame oil
sriracha sauce, to taste

Bursting with flavour and so, so good, largely thanks to two extremely tasty sauces. Originating from Hawaii, Poke is raw fish salad, or 'sushi in a bowl' by any other description. Typically, top quality raw fish, such as tuna or salmon, is marinated and arranged over bowls of sushi rice, alongside fresh and pickled vegetables, avocado and spicy mayonnaise. Anything goes (the ingredients are variable), so poke bowls are a good way of using up leftover vegetables, cooked meat and poultry. Try tofu for a change, and don't forget the chopsticks!

1. Put the rice into a small pan with 180ml of cold water, put the lid on and bring to the boil. Lower the heat and simmer very gently for 13 minutes. Remove from the heat and leave to steam for 10 minutes with the lid on. Remove the lid and stir in the rice/rice wine vinegar. Divide between two bowls.

2. Meanwhile, cook the edamame beans in a separate small pan of boiling well-salted water for 3 minutes, then drain and cool.

3. Mix the marinade ingredients together in a small mixing bowl and stir in the salmon. Set aside. Mix the sauce ingredients together in a separate small bowl and set aside.

4. Arrange the carrot, edamame beans and pickled cucumber (or other pickles), with a little of its juice, in groups over the rice around the edge of the bowls. Then add the salmon, with its marinade, in the same way. Remove the avocado halves from their skin with a large spoon, fan out the slices and arrange on the rice.

5. Drizzle the sauce in lines over the top of the bowls, or spoon it into the bowls. Scatter with the spring onions and some toasted sesame seeds. Serve.

GET AHEAD

• The rice can be cooked the day before. Cool quickly, cover and chill, then serve cold, or reheat to serve (reheat until hot throughout). The edamame beans, carrot, pickled cucumber and spring onions can be prepared the day before, as can the marinade and sauce; cover and chill separately.

HINTS & TIPS

• Traditionally, the rice is served warm and the toppings at room temperature. However, the rice doesn't have to be warm, it can be served hot or cold.

• I love making poke bowls for picnics. They can be prepared in advance, are very transportable, and everyone has their own container.

Fettuccine Alfredo

SERVES 2

200g dried fettuccine (or tagliatelle)
salt and freshly ground black pepper
150ml double cream
20g butter
a generous grating of nutmeg,
  plus extra to serve
100g Parmesan cheese, grated
  (see tip on page 17)
freshly chopped parsley, to finish
  (optional)

GET AHEAD

• The sauce ingredients can be
  mixed together in a bowl or jug
  any time on the day (keep at room
  temperature), ready to add to the
  pan and warm through once the
  pasta is drained.

HINTS & TIPS

• Cooked chicken, ham, bacon
  or mushrooms could be added
  to the sauce before incorporating
  the pasta. When in season, I also
  like to add some cooked, chopped
  (preferably British) asparagus spears.

This is a luscious, creamy hug in a bowl achieved with surprisingly few ingredients, most of which are store cupboard staples. Roughly based on a recipe named after a Roman restaurateur, this is a comforting and indulgent treat. For vegetarians, swap the Parmesan for a vegetarian Italian-style hard cheese.

1. Add the fettuccine to a large pan of boiling very well-salted water and cook according to the packet instructions. Scoop out and reserve a cupful of the cooking water and then drain the pasta.

2. Using the pasta pan, heat the cream, butter, nutmeg, Parmesan and a little seasoning together on a low heat, stirring, until warmed through. Check the seasoning.

3. Return the pasta to the pan and stir to coat and blanket all the strands individually with the sauce, adding some of the reserved pasta water, little by little, to loosen the sauce, as necessary. As it cools it will thicken up. Divide between two bowls and serve immediately, topped with an extra grating of nutmeg and some parsley (if using) to finish.

From the Oven

Some of these recipes are speedy in their preparation, rather than in their cooking. Longer cooking has the advantage of freeing up time to get on with other things while the oven works its magic. Since the oven's doing the work, I consider these still to be time-savers in their way. I have included some roasts as I think they enter most people's lives at some stage throughout the year. You'll find that some recipes are worth cooking for the smells that permeate the kitchen alone!

Roasted Duck Leg & Fennel Boulangère with Orange Gremolata

SERVES 4

700g potatoes, such as Maris Piper, peeled or unpeeled (I don't peel!)
2 fennel bulbs, tough outer layer and stems discarded, halved through the root, green fronds reserved
1 onion, halved through the root
1½ teaspoons fennel seeds, roughly crushed or coarsely ground
1½ teaspoons salt, plus extra for sprinkling
freshly ground black pepper
150ml chicken stock (or use ½ stock cube)
4 duck legs, well trimmed of excess skin and fat

For the orange gremolata
a good handful of parsley (10–15g), tough stalks discarded
1 fat garlic clove, peeled
grated zest of 1 orange (and the juice squeezed, optional)

This rustic one-pan dish of classic boulangère potatoes (with the addition of fennel) cooked with duck legs sitting on top, is jazzed up with zingy orange gremolata at the end. Gremolata is so good for enlivening all sorts of things. Here, I have swapped the traditional lemon zest for orange to complement the duck. A comforting and very tasty recipe!

1. Preheat the oven to 230°C/210°C fan/gas 8. Find a deepish ovenproof dish into which the duck legs will just fit in one layer (I use a round 29 x 6cm dish).

2. Slice the potatoes, fennel and onion thinly using the slicing blade of a food-processor, a mandolin or by hand. Transfer them to a large bowl and mix well with the fennel seeds, the measured salt and some black pepper. Hands are easiest for this. Tip the vegetables into the ovenproof dish and level the top. Pour over the stock. Arrange the duck legs on top of the potatoes and sprinkle lightly with salt.

3. Put the dish into the oven, turn it down to 220°C/200°C fan/gas 7 and roast for 1¼ hours, until the duck legs are crisp and golden and the potatoes are soft and tender when pierced all the way through with a knife.

4. While the duck is cooking, prepare the gremolata. Finely chop the parsley, garlic and reserved fennel fronds together, then mix in the orange zest at the end.

5. Remove the duck and veg from the oven and pour the orange juice (if using) over the potatoes. Leave to cool down for 20 minutes or so before serving – if steam is still in evidence when the dish is dug into, it will taste of nothing. Scatter the gremolata over the potatoes and serve with a lightly cooked green vegetable, a leafy green salad or some watercress.

GET AHEAD

• Complete step 2 up to an hour before cooking and keep at room temperature. The gremolata can be made any time on the day, covered and set aside until required.

• The cooked dish (without the gremolata) can be kept warm for an hour or so before serving.

HINTS & TIPS

• Switch the garlic in the gremolata for a finely chopped small shallot, if you prefer, and swap grated lemon zest for the orange zest (but not the lemon juice for the orange juice).

Baked Whole Salmon Fillet with Tarragon & Lime

SERVES 4–5

olive oil, for drizzling
650g salmon fillet in one piece,
  skin on or off
sea salt flakes and freshly ground
  black pepper
1 teaspoon dried tarragon
a few dried chilli flakes (optional)
4 teaspoons small capers in brine,
  drained
juice of 1 lime
40g butter, for dotting
a small handful of parsley,
  leaves roughly chopped

HINTS & TIPS

• The salmon can be served hot or
  cold. If serving cold, drizzle with
  olive oil in place of dotting with the
  butter before cooking. The butter
  will set hard when cold and be
  unpalatable, whereas olive oil
  will produce a tasty dressing-style
  sauce with the lime juice, capers
  and salmon juices.

• Accompaniments are endless
  and include: boiled new or creamy
  mashed potatoes, cooked noodles,
  rice or orzo; lightly cooked green
  vegetables, such as pak choi,
  spinach, tenderstem broccoli,
  French beans; green and other
  salads; mayonnaise, flavoured
  mayonnaise (such as watercress),
  foaming hollandaise sauce,
  salsa verde.

Such an easy way of cooking salmon and lovely to put in the middle of the table for everyone to help themselves. This recipe produces juicy succulent salmon and is easily upped for more people – just buy a larger fillet and extend the cooking time by a few minutes. Salmon is filling, so you need less than you might think.

Served lukewarm, or at room temperature with mayonnaise and new potatoes, this makes a delicious summer recipe, too.

1. Preheat the oven to 200°C/180°C fan/gas 6. Line a small, shallow roasting tin slightly bigger than the piece of salmon with baking parchment, allowing enough to reach up the sides (scrunching up and then opening out the paper first makes this much easier). Grease the middle section with a splash of olive oil.

2. Put the salmon into the tin, drizzle with a little olive oil and scatter with some salt and pepper, the tarragon, chilli flakes (if using) and capers. Pour over the lime juice, dot the butter all over the salmon and then scatter with the parsley.

3. Bake for 10–12 minutes until the salmon is slightly undercooked in the very middle. It will continue cooking when removed from the oven. Immediately slide the fish, on its baking parchment, onto a serving plate or board and keep somewhere warm to rest for 10 minutes before serving. Up to 30 minutes or so resting is fine. Ensure everyone gets some of the delicious buttery juices when serving themselves.

Spicy One-pan 'Spanish' Chicken Bake

SERVES 4

1 large fennel bulb, tough outer
  layer and stems discarded (fronds
  reserved – optional), cut into
  8 wedges through the root,
  then across into chunks
1 large red pepper, quartered,
  de-seeded, then each quarter cut
  into 3 chunks
1 onion, cut into 8 wedges through
  the root, then across into chunks
500g waxy new/salad potatoes,
  cut into roughly 1cm-thick slices
1 garlic bulb, cloves separated
  and left unpeeled
about 20 pitted black olives
8 even-sized chicken thighs,
  skin-on, bone-in, well trimmed
  of excess skin and fat
sea salt flakes
olive oil, for drizzling

For the marinade
1 tablespoon sherry vinegar
2 tablespoons olive oil
1 teaspoon hot smoked paprika
1 teaspoon salt
good grinding of freshly ground
  black pepper
1 teaspoon dried oregano

This can't really be called Spanish, but some of the ingredients are typically used in Spanish cuisine so the name is used loosely. The finished dish isn't meant to be swimming in sauce but the juices are very tasty, so ensure everyone gets some! Once the vegetables are chunked up, the oven does all the work.

1. Preheat the oven to 220°C/200°C fan/gas 7. Find a shallow roasting tin (around 35 x 26 x 4cm – try to stick to roughly this size to ensure the delicious juices are produced).

2. Put the vegetables, garlic cloves and olives into the roasting tin. In a small bowl, mix all the marinade ingredients together, then pour this over the vegetables and stir well with a wooden spoon to coat everything evenly. Level out in the tin, ensuring everything is evenly distributed.

3. Sit the chicken thighs on top (they shouldn't be touching), sprinkle with a little salt and a drizzle of olive oil and cook at the very top of the oven for 35 minutes. Remove from the oven, jiggle the vegetables between the thighs around a little, turn the tray round and put back into the oven for a further 20 minutes or until the chicken skin is golden and crisp.

4. Serve from the tin, scattered with the reserved fennel fronds (if using) and a leafy green salad, if you like.

GET AHEAD

• The fennel, red pepper, onion and garlic can be prepared any time on the day; the potatoes can be prepared up to an hour before cooking (keep all at room temperature). The chicken thighs can be trimmed a day or two in advance, covered and chilled.

• The marinade can be made up to 3 days in advance, covered and kept at room temperature. Don't add to the vegetables until just before cooking.

HINTS & TIPS

• If time is short, use a whole roasted red pepper from a jar, drained and cut into chunks.

Cod Loin Fillets with Courgette 'Frites'

SERVES 2

1 tablespoon plain flour
sea salt flakes and freshly ground
    black pepper
350g small firm courgettes
    (a couple or so more if you
    like, they are very moreish!)
1 tablespoon olive oil, plus extra
    for drizzling
2 cod loins (or fillets), about
    150g each, skinned
a squeeze of fresh lemon juice
    (optional)

GET AHEAD

• The recipe can be completed up to
  the end of step 5 any time on the
  day and left at room temperature.
  Continue with step 6 just before
  eating.

HINTS & TIPS

• Optional flavourings to add to the
  flour include: 2 tablespoons grated
  Parmesan cheese (see tip on page
  17); good pinch of smoked paprika,
  hot smoked paprika or ground
  cumin; a few dried chilli flakes.

• Swap cod for other fish fillets, such
  as haddock, hake, sea bass or sea
  bream (skin on or off).

• Bear in mind that loins and thicker
  fillets will take a few minutes longer
  to cook.

An easy, tasty supper cooked on one tray. This courgette version of frites, or skinny fries, although mainly golden and crisp, won't be quite as crunchy as the potato kind. The courgette doubter to whom I'm married, is in no doubt about his love of these! It's best to use small, firm courgettes, and I wouldn't attempt this for more than two people. See *Hints & Tips* for different flavouring suggestions.

1. Preheat the oven to 220°C/200°C fan/gas 7. Find a baking tray around 37 x 27cm, preferably non-stick, but lightly greased if not.

2. In a largish bowl, mix together the flour, a little salt and a twist of black pepper (and any other dry flavourings, if using – see *Hints & Tips*).

3. Cut the courgettes into sections around 7cm long and then into batons around (but no thinner than) 1cm. If using medium to large courgettes, discard the middle batons made up of the soft seedy central core, as they'll just become soggy and floppy.

4. Add the courgettes to the flour in the bowl and toss until they're all lightly coated and the flour is absorbed, then add the oil and toss again until it's absorbed and all the courgettes are coated.

5. Spread out in one layer on the baking tray and cook at the top of the oven for around 15 minutes, until golden on the underside, then turn over and cook for another 5–8 minutes or so, until mostly brown all over.

6. Push the courgettes towards one end of the tray to allow just enough space for the cod. Grease with a smidgen of oil, if necessary, put the cod onto the tray, drizzle with a little olive oil and season, then return to the oven for 5–7 minutes or until just cooked through (cod loins will take a little longer than fillets).

7. Transfer the cod to two plates and pile the courgettes on top. Serve immediately with a drizzle of olive oil and a squeeze of lemon juice, if you like. Some boiled new potatoes would be good alongside and possibly a dollop of pesto sauce (see notes on page 17) or Chimichurri (see page 75) or Salsa Verde (see page 76).

Roasted Ham Shank

SERVES 3–4

1 ham shank, around 1.5kg

HINTS & TIPS

• Accompaniments include: Crisp
Herby Potato Wedges (see page
152), Creamy Baked Parmesan
Potatoes (see page 151), baked
or mashed potatoes; cabbage of
any sort, cooked in any way; other
lightly cooked green vegetables; a
vegetable in white sauce, such as
broad beans; sauerkraut (available
ready-made in jars).

Over the years, I have probably cooked this for our day-to-day eating
more than anything else. It's my husband John's absolute favourite. Eaten
hot the first time around, what's left over then sits in the fridge (for up
to 3 days, or a little longer), ready to be used in all manner of recipes, as
well as sandwiches and for general snacking. It never goes to waste. In fact,
because of this versatility, I mostly cook two shanks at a time.

Ham shanks are inexpensive, freeze well uncooked, and are almost always
sold smoked. The meat is delectably tender, sticky and flavoursome and,
as an added bonus, the skin transforms into a sort of crackling.

1. Preheat the oven to 200°C/180°C fan/gas 6.

2. Put the ham shank into a small, shallow roasting tin (lined with foil
if you'd like to save on washing up) and roast in the oven for 2 hours.

3. Remove from the oven and allow the ham to rest for 10–15 minutes
before serving, although kept somewhere warm, considerably longer is
fine. Serve as is, or with Cumberland or Mustard Sauce (see below) or
parsley sauce.

Cumberland Sauce

Heat the juice from 1 lemon and 1 orange with 1 teaspoon of English
mustard powder, 6 drops of Tabasco sauce and a pinch of salt in a small
saucepan on a low heat, stirring, until dissolved. Stir in 100ml of ruby
port and 115g of redcurrant jelly, bring to the boil, then reduce the heat
and simmer for 10–15 minutes until the redcurrant jelly has dissolved.
Traditionally served cold, this is just as good served warm.

Mustard Sauce

Stir 1 tablespoon each of whole grain (seedy) mustard and Dijon mustard
into 150g of crème fraîche and spoon into a small serving bowl. Alternatively,
heat the sauce gently in a saucepan before serving warm.

Butternut Squash, Lentils & Halloumi with Mint & Garlic Sauce

SERVES 4

1 butternut squash, around 800g
  total weight, peeled, de-seeded
  and cut into wedges/boats around
  3cm thick at the fattest point
1 small-medium onion, cut into
  8 wedges through the root
1 small-medium red onion,
  cut into 8 wedges through the root
1 teaspoon ras el hanout
salt and freshly ground black pepper
olive oil, for drizzling
1 x 250g pouch of ready-cooked
  Puy lentils
225–250g halloumi cheese, cut into
  8–10 x 1cm slices
dried chilli flakes, to taste

For the mint and garlic sauce
175g thick Greek-style yoghurt
a handful of chopped mint leaves
1 small garlic clove, crushed
salt and freshly ground black pepper

A colourful and healthy vegetarian main course (ensure to choose halloumi that is vegetarian) that can be prepared well in advance and takes only a few minutes to finish off when required. There's plenty of scope for switching the vegetables to make use of what you have to hand. I like to serve this from the tin, but by all means decant it to a platter, if you prefer.

1. Preheat the oven to 220°C/200°C fan/gas 7.

2. Put the squash and onions into a shallow roasting tin, around 41 x 26cm and ideally no deeper than 4cm (or use a large, lipped baking tray). Sprinkle with the ras el hanout, some salt and pepper and a good glug of olive oil. Mix everything together to coat evenly, shake the tin to level the ingredients out in one layer, then roast at the top of the oven for 25 minutes.

3. Mix the sauce ingredients together in a small serving bowl and set aside. Turn the grill on to its highest setting.

4. Remove the tin from the oven and carefully turn over the vegetables – some will be charred and some won't – scatter the lentils over evenly, then shake the tin to distribute them into the nooks and crannies. Return to the oven for another 5 minutes.

5. Arrange the halloumi slices over the vegetables, sprinkle them with a few chilli flakes and drizzle with a little olive oil. Place the tin under the grill, as high up as it will go, and grill for 5 minutes or until the halloumi is golden brown in places and softened. Drizzle over a little more olive oil and serve from the tin, with the mint and garlic sauce.

GET AHEAD

• Complete to the end of step 3 (don't turn on the grill) up to 2 days in advance, cool, cover and chill the veg (cover and chill the sauce). If your tin is non-stick, the veg can be stored in the tin. To continue with step 4, add the lentils to the tin and allow 10 minutes in the oven (at the same temp) for all the vegetables to heat up before adding the halloumi and continuing as above.

HINTS & TIPS

• For a vegan version, use vegan halloumi-style cheese (or omit the cheese altogether) and use coconut yoghurt for the sauce.

• This is lovely enjoyed as a salad as well, served at room temperature.

Baked Whole Sea Bream with Hazelnut & Parsley Relish

SERVES 2

2 whole sea bream, about 400g
  each, cleaned, scaled, fins removed
  (ask the fishmonger to do this)
1 lemon
a few thyme sprigs
a few parsley sprigs
butter, for dotting
salt and freshly ground black pepper
olive oil, for drizzling

For the hazelnut and parsley relish
55g blanched hazelnuts, toasted
  (see *Get Ahead* tip on page 35)
2 handfuls of parsley leaves
  (around 25g)
1 garlic clove, roughly chopped
¼ teaspoon salt
generous grinding of black pepper
6 tablespoons (90ml) olive oil

Whole sea bream (and sea bass) are widely available and make a lovely simple supper if you enjoy leisurely picking over bones, as we do. If that's not your thing, use fillets instead and reduce the baking time to 5 minutes. Swap sea bass for the bream, if you like.

1. Preheat the oven to 200°C/180°C fan/gas 6. Line a shallow roasting tin, just large enough to fit the bream side-by-side, with baking parchment.

2. Whizz all the relish ingredients, minus the olive oil, together in a small food-processor bowl until finely but chunkily chopped, then add and whizz in the olive oil. Check the seasoning, it may need a little more salt. The relish will be a thick, spooning consistency, rather than a pouring consistency. Add more olive oil if you prefer a runnier version. Set aside.

3. Slash three cuts into the top of each fish, right down to the bone, and place them in the lined tin. Cut the lemon in half, around its girth. Squeeze the juice from one half, then cut the remaining piece in half and then into thin slices, producing triangular slivers. Insert a sliver into each of the cuts on top of the fish, rind uppermost, and divide the remainder between the cavities, along with the herb sprigs and a small knob of butter.

4. Pour the lemon juice over the fish, followed by some seasoning. Dot with a little butter and a drizzle of olive oil, then bake at the top of the oven for 15–20 minutes until just cooked through. Serve with the cooking juices spooned over, and some relish – and a bit-bowl!

GET AHEAD

- The bream can be prepared to the end of step 3 any time on the day, covered and kept in the fridge. Bring back to room temperature an hour or so before cooking.

- Step 2 can be made up to 3 days in advance. The relish (there will be some left over) will keep for several weeks in the fridge, stored in a covered jar or bowl with a slick of olive oil over the top. It can also be frozen (defrost before use).

HINTS & TIPS

- When it's in season, I swap wild garlic leaves for the parsley in the fish cavities, and in the relish, too.

- This recipe is easily doubled, just allow a little longer cooking time.

- One slightly larger sea bream will feed two people; it will take a bit longer to cook.

Roast Haggis-stuffed Chicken

SERVES 5–6

butter, softened, for
  greasing and smearing
1 x 400g haggis
1.7kg whole chicken,
  untrussed, excess fatty bits
  removed from the cavity
salt and freshly ground
  black pepper
6 rashers streaky bacon
  (smoked or unsmoked)
plain flour, for thickening

GET AHEAD

• The chicken can be stuffed the
  day before, covered and chilled.
  Bring it back to room temperature
  2 hours before cooking.

HINTS & TIPS

• Vegetable water, a splash of red
  or white wine or some stock (or
  a little of all three) can be added
  to the gravy instead of simply
  using all water, if you like.

• For a larger or smaller chicken,
  the cooking time will need adjusting.
  Also adjust the quantity of haggis
  used, ensuring the chicken is fully
  stuffed for each option – if using a
  smaller chicken, you could roll the
  excess haggis into golf ball-sized
  balls and cook alongside the chicken,
  then remove from the tin at the same
  time as the bacon and then later add
  to the resting chicken with the bacon
  as above (or freeze any leftover
  uncooked haggis for another use).

This is one of the tastiest of stuffings, and the easiest, too, being ready-made. Savoury, peppery and flavourful, haggis makes a lovely stuffing and complements the mild flavour of chicken beautifully. Some people are unsure about haggis (usually the ones that haven't tasted it), so I would advise referring to it simply as 'stuffing'! The chicken needs to rest for at least 30 minutes after cooking, so bear this in mind when calculating timings.

1. Preheat the oven to 220°C/200°C fan/gas 7. Find a shallow roasting tin just a little bit larger than the chicken (too big and the juices will burn, which will spoil the gravy – this goes for all roasts) and very lightly butter the base.

2. Slit the haggis casing lengthways, break the haggis into sections and stuff it into the cavity of the chicken. It'll be quite a squash, but it will all go in. Use the flaps of skin at the top of the cavity opening to partly enclose the outermost section of haggis. Discard the casing.

3. Put the chicken into the roasting tin, season, then smear the skin all over with a little butter. Arrange the bacon rashers over the chicken, slightly overlapping each other across (and covering) the breast.

4. Slide the chicken into the top of the oven, reduce the temperature to 200°C/180°C fan/gas 6, and roast for 1¼ hours. Remove the bacon after 25–30 minutes or when it's crisp, and transfer to a plate. Baste the chicken and return it to the oven for the remaining cooking time. Carefully transfer the chicken to a cold plate, leave to sit for 5 minutes, then add the cooked bacon to the same plate and keep somewhere warm for a minimum of 30 minutes (up to an hour is fine).

5. Skim off and discard all but roughly 1 tablespoon of fat from the roasting tin, being careful to leave the cooking juices behind, and mix in enough flour (around 2 tablespoons) to soak up the fat and make a roux (I use a fish slice for making gravy). Gradually incorporate enough cold water (see *Hints & Tips*) into the roux, stirring until it has blended into a lump-free liquid. Add a little more water (you'll need around 400–500ml of water in all) and some seasoning, bring the gravy to the boil on a medium heat, stirring continuously, and simmer for a few minutes. If the gravy is too thick, add a little more cold water. Check the seasoning. Pour the gravy into a warmed jug or sauceboat.

6. Carve the chicken and serve with some of the haggis stuffing and the bacon. Bread sauce and peas are must-have accompaniments for me, as well as roast or mashed potatoes.

Roast Spatchcock Poussins with 'Nduja Butter

SERVES 4

60g butter, softened, plus
   a little extra for greasing
60g 'nduja paste
4 x 400g (single) or
   2 x 500g poussins
salt and freshly ground
   black pepper
a handful of parsley, roughly
   chopped, to serve (optional)

GET AHEAD

- Complete to the end of step 2 any time on the day. Loosely cover the poussins and keep somewhere cool.

- The 'nduja butter can be made up to 3 days in advance and kept covered in the fridge, although longer is fine. Bring back to room temperature before smearing it over the birds. It can also be frozen (defrost before use).

HINTS & TIPS

- Try 'nduja butter slathered over hot new potatoes and other cooked vegetables, spread on toast and canapé bases, or melted over poached or fried eggs, hot steaks and grilled fish.

The beauty of spatchcocked birds is they have a shorter cooking time than a whole bird, and offer a larger surface area of tasty skin. 'Nduja is a very flavourful Italian spreadable salami with a spicy kick to it. The paste version used here is available from most large supermarkets or online. This recipe is easily halved and can also be made using a whole chicken. Poussins come in two sizes – small, as a single serving, and slightly larger, which serves two. They are very succulent and tender, make a lovely small-scale mid-week roast and are great for entertaining.

1. Preheat the oven to 230°C/210°C fan/gas 8. Find a shallow roasting tin into which the spatchcocked birds will fit, allowing a little space around each one, and lightly butter the base.

2. Mix together the 60g of butter and the 'nduja paste in a small bowl. Turn the poussins upside down onto their breasts and cut along either side of the backbone (i.e. either side of the parson's nose) with scissors, then remove and discard the backbones, as well as any excess pieces of fat on the underside. Turn the poussins over and press down hard on each breast with the heel of your hand to flatten the poussin. Put the poussins into the roasting tin, with their drumstick bones parallel and next door to each other, and smear the 'nduja butter all over the skin of each bird, getting into all the nooks and crannies.

3. Season the poussins, slide the tin into the top of the oven, reduce the oven temperature to 220°C/200°C fan/gas 7 and roast for 25 minutes, until the skin is golden brown and the poussins are cooked through. Remove to a plate and rest somewhere warm for 15 minutes (longer is fine). Decant the buttery cooking juices and sticky bits from the bottom of the tin into a small jug and keep warm.

4. Arrange the poussins on a serving platter (if cooking two larger poussins, cut them in half), scatter with chopped parsley (if using) and serve.

- Serving suggestions include: boiled new or mashed potatoes; cooked plain rice (or pre-mixed cooked Basmati and wild rice) and a lightly cooked green vegetable and/or green salad.

Haddock, Potato & Fennel Bake with Parma Ham Crisps & Pesto

SERVES 4

1–2 tablespoons olive oil, plus
  extra for greasing and drizzling
750g waxy new/salad potatoes,
  cut into ½cm-thick rounds
2 fennel bulbs, tough outer layer
  and stems discarded (fronds
  reserved – optional), halved
  through the root and cut into
  roughly ½cm slices
sea salt flakes and freshly
  ground black pepper
4 slices Parma ham, halved
  (cutting with scissors through
  the ham and it's dividing paper
  together is easiest)
2 tablespoons pesto sauce,
  or more to taste (see notes
  on page 17)
500g skinless haddock fillet(s),
  cut into 8 pieces in total

GET AHEAD

• Complete to the end of step 2 any
  time on the day, cool, loosely cover
  and keep at room temperature.
  Reheat the vegetables in their tin
  (temp as above) for 8–10 minutes
  or until sizzling, before adding the
  haddock and continuing as above.

• Step 3 can be completed any
  time on the day and kept at
  room temperature.

An easy 'bung it in the oven' supper! Everything can be prepared ahead, leaving only a few minutes' cooking before serving. The Parma ham crisps on top are optional but well worth it. We absolutely love this.

1. Preheat the oven to 230°C/210°C fan/gas 8. Lightly grease a large, shallow roasting tin, around 41 x 26 x 4cm (or use a large, lipped baking tray) with olive oil.

2. Spread the potatoes out in the tin, roughly in a single layer, and evenly scatter over the fennel slices. Swirl with a generous drizzle of olive oil and season with salt and pepper. Slide the tin into the top of the oven, reduce the temperature to 220°C/200°C fan/gas 7 and roast for 25 minutes. Remove from the oven and turn the potatoes and fennel over with a fish slice – some of them will be golden and crispy, some won't, and some might stick and break up a little, all of which is fine. Return to the oven for another 10 minutes.

3. Meanwhile, heat a small splash of olive oil in a medium (preferably non-stick) frying pan. Scrunch up each piece of Parma ham with your fingertips by gripping the middle, to create a sort of crumpled frilly rose/pompom. Add to the pan, flat-side down, and cook on a high heat for a few minutes until golden and crisp, then turn over and repeat. Drain on kitchen paper and set aside.

4. In a small bowl, loosen the pesto to a pouring consistency with the tablespoon or two of olive oil and set aside.

5. Arrange the haddock pieces in a single layer on top of the vegetables, season and drizzle them with olive oil, top each one with a Parma ham crisp and then return to the oven for a further 5–7 minutes, until the fish is opaque and just cooked through.

6. You may like to drizzle a little pesto sauce over each piece of fish, or serve the sauce separately. Scatter the fish with the roughly chopped reserved fennel fronds (if using) and serve from the tin.

Roast Dukkah Rack of Lamb with Pea & Mint Salsa & Redcurrant Sauce

SERVES 4–6

olive oil, for greasing and drizzling
2 racks of lamb (6–7 cutlets on
  each), chined and French-trimmed
  (the butcher will do this for you),
  trimmed of skin and excess fat
4 teaspoons dukkah
salt

For the redcurrant sauce
2 tablespoons redcurrant jelly
2 tablespoons red wine vinegar
300ml lamb or chicken stock (or use
  1 x 28g stock pot or a stock cube)

For the salsa
200g frozen peas
2 spring onions, trimmed
  and roughly sliced
8 mint leaves
2½ tablespoons olive oil
1 tablespoon cider or
  white wine vinegar
½ teaspoon salt

I think of rack of lamb as something special and like to serve it when entertaining. Here, the lamb is accompanied by a very quick vibrant-green salsa and an equally speedy sauce. A great get-ahead recipe for when you have guests.

1. Preheat the oven to 220°C/200°C fan/gas 7. Lightly grease a small-medium, shallow roasting tin with a smidgen of olive oil.

2. Lay the lamb racks flat in the roasting tin, fat-side up, rub a little olive oil into the fat and then sprinkle over and press 2 teaspoons of dukkah into each rack. Sprinkle them with a little salt and a small drizzle of olive oil. Roast at the top of the oven for 18–20 minutes for pink lamb (or roast for a little longer if you prefer your lamb less pink). Transfer the lamb to a cold plate and leave somewhere warm to rest (such as in a low oven with the door ajar).

3. Meanwhile, make the redcurrant sauce. Put all the ingredients into a small saucepan and bring to the boil on a low-medium heat, then simmer until reduced by about half. Pour into a serving jug and keep warm.

4. Make the salsa. Put the peas into a small saucepan with a pinch of salt, barely cover with boiling water from the kettle and bring just to the boil. Drain immediately. Whizz the peas with all the remaining salsa ingredients to a purée using a stick blender or in the smallest bowl of a food-processor. It will retain a little texture. Transfer to a bowl (it's not meant to be hot).

5. Slice the rested lamb into cutlets, arrange on a serving platter and serve the salsa separately, or serve the cutlets on individual plates with some of the salsa alongside, if you like. Serve the redcurrant sauce separately with both options.

GET AHEAD

- Seasoning the lamb racks with olive oil and dukkah in step 2 can be done any time on the day, then kept covered somewhere cool, but don't finish off with the salt and olive oil until ready to roast.

- Step 3 can be made up to 3 days in advance, cooled, covered and chilled, then reheated gently when required. It can also be frozen.

- Step 4 can be made up to 3 days in advance, however, drain the peas and cool under cold running water before making the salsa. Don't add the vinegar until an hour or so before serving. Cover and keep chilled. Bring back to room temperature to serve.

- The longer the lamb has to rest, the better. Up to an hour (or more) is fine, as long as you keep it warm.

HINTS & TIPS

- Serve with potatoes, such as Hasselback Potatoes (see page 144), Crisp Herby Potato Wedges (see page 152), Creamy Baked Parmesan Potatoes (see page 151), boiled new potatoes or roast potatoes, and a lightly cooked green vegetable.

Speedy Sides & Salads

Rather than green vegetables, which generally only take minutes to cook and are often best left unadulterated, thus not requiring a recipe, I have mostly concentrated on other vegetables in this chapter. These recipes are quick to prepare and can largely be cooked in advance.

To cook (most) green vegetables, put them in a saucepan with a good pinch of salt, barely cover with boiling water and simmer (no lid) for a few minutes until just tender, then drain and briefly refresh under cold water. Alternatively, steam the vegetables.

Hasselback Potatoes

SERVES 8 (depending
on size of potatoes)

24–32 small waxy new potatoes,
   such as Charlotte
good glug of olive oil
good knob of butter
salt
2 rosemary sprigs, leaves picked
   and roughly chopped (optional)

A cross between sauté and roast potatoes, but with a lot less effort, these tasty Swedish potatoes go so well with most things – fish, poultry, meat, sausages and vegetables, particularly when fried, grilled or barbecued. They can be adorned with myriad toppings, either before cooking or just before serving. Suitable for vegetarians.

1. Preheat the oven to 200°C/180°C fan/gas 6.

2. Sit a potato lengthways in the bowl of a wooden spoon (this prevents slicing all the way through it). Make cuts, 2mm apart, across the potato until you hit the wooden spoon. Repeat with all the potatoes.

3. Gently heat the olive oil and butter in a shallow roasting tin (just big enough to take the potatoes in one layer without being crammed in (but not so big that parts of the tin are empty), add the prepped potatoes, then roll and swish around to coat them all in fat. Ensure they're all sitting cut-side-up, then sprinkle with a little salt and the rosemary (if using).

4. Roast at the top of the oven for 40–55 minutes or until golden brown all over, basting halfway through (if you remember) and turning over for the last 5–10 minutes or so to brown the tops, if necessary. Serve the potatoes as they are, or with any of the topping suggestions (see *Hints & Tips*).

GET AHEAD

- Step 2 can be done any time on the day and the potatoes kept submerged in a bowl of cold water. When required, drain and dry well on kitchen paper. They may take a little longer to cook, especially if not completely dry.

- If the roasted potatoes (step 4) are ready before needed, remove the tin from the oven and set aside at room temperature, then return to the oven (temp as above) for 5–10 minutes to reheat and crisp up, when required.

HINTS & TIPS

- No wooden spoon? Sit each potato between two chopsticks placed on the worktop, or thread a skewer horizontally through each potato, close to the bottom, then make the cuts as above until you hit the chopsticks/skewer.

- Hasselbacks work just as well with maincrop potatoes, but they may take a little longer to cook. Halve any very big ones before slicing, then slice and cook them with the flat, cut-side down.

- Filling and topping ideas: herb sprigs and/or garlic slices pushed into the cuts; dried chilli flakes; cheese (creamy, grated hard or crumbled blue); flavoured butters, such as sriracha, garlic, herb or shallot; pestos; salsas, such as salsa verde; flavoured yoghurt sauces; gremolata; tapenade; crispy bacon . . .

Celeriac Chips

SERVES 4

1 small celeriac, about 500–600g
olive oil, for drizzling
sea salt flakes and freshly
ground black pepper

GET AHEAD

• If the chips are ready before you
need them, leave them in the tin
and heat up to sizzling again in
the oven (temp as above) for a
few minutes just before serving.

• The recipe can be completed the
day before, cooled, covered and
chilled, then reheated (temp as
above) until hot and sizzling.

HINTS & TIPS

• The weight given for the celeriac
is just a guide. Don't be put off
using a whole bulb if it's heavier,
just use a bigger tin so the chips
aren't crammed in.

• When adding the seasoning in
step 4, try also scattering over a
good pinch of any of the following:
smoked paprika, hot smoked paprika,
curry powder (any strength), ground
cumin, Aleppo pepper (pul biber)
or dried herbs, or 1–2 tablespoons
of finely grated Parmesan cheese
(see tip on page 17).

Celeriac chips are far tastier than you might think and surprisingly
moreish. In fact, I could polish off an indecent amount in one sitting!
They aren't as crisp as deep-fried potato chips, but will be crisp in places
and nicely caramelised. Celeriac is lower in carbs than potatoes and is just
about as versatile. I've suggested some coatings (see *Hints & Tips*), which
can be added before cooking. I particularly enjoy celeriac chips with fish,
although they're good with just about everything, or simply on their own
dipped into mayo. Suitable for vegetarians and vegans.

1. Preheat the oven to 220°C/200°C fan/gas 7.

2. Slice the top and bottom off the celeriac using a large knife, then cut the
skin off thinly with the knife following the contours of the bulb and trying
not to waste the flesh.

3. Cut the bulb into slices around 1cm thick, and then into long chips of
around the same thickness. Depending on the size of the bulb, cut the chips
in half or into thirds or to the length you like. They won't all be (and don't
need to be) the same length.

4. Spread the chips out in a shallow roasting tin (or baking tray) large
enough to fit them so they're quite well spaced apart in a single layer,
to ensure browning. Drizzle with a little olive oil, just enough to lightly
coat the chips, sprinkle over some salt and pepper, mix together to coat
the chips and then shake the tin so they're in a single layer.

5. Bake at the top of the oven for 15–20 minutes, until golden brown
underneath and they will lift from the tin willingly, then turn over and
bake for about 5 more minutes, until golden brown and caramelised.
Serve immediately.

Shaved Courgette, Fennel & Mint Salad

SERVES 4
(as a side salad)

2 firm medium courgettes,
  or more, smaller, ones
  (around 325g total weight)
1 small fennel bulb, tough outer
  layer and stems removed
  (fronds reserved), halved
  and shaved with a mandolin
2 mint sprigs, leaves picked and
  stacked, rolled into a tight
  'cigarette' and very finely
  sliced into ribbons
½ tablespoon olive oil
juice of ½ lemon
½ teaspoon sea salt flakes,
  or to taste
freshly ground black pepper

HINTS & TIPS

• Omit the fennel, if you prefer.

I make this on repeat during the summer with our (inevitable) courgette glut. Quick, fresh and very tasty, it always hits the spot and goes well with almost anything – hot or cold. The salad looks particularly pretty with different coloured and shaped courgettes. Try serving it with grilled or baked fillets of fish and some buttery boiled baby new potatoes. Suitable for vegetarians and vegans.

1. Using a potato peeler, peel off (lengthways) and discard three strips of skin at intervals from around each courgette, creating a striped effect. Into a mixing bowl, peel/shave the courgettes into long ribbons, working around the courgette after every shaving, thus creating wide ribbons with thin strips of green skin down each side. Stop when you get to the core of seeds in the middle and discard this.

2. Add all the remaining ingredients. Lightly and quickly toss together (hands are best) and check the seasoning. Arrange on a serving platter (leaving any excess liquid behind), scatter with the reserved snipped fennel fronds and serve immediately.

Creamy Baked Parmesan Potatoes

500g waxy salad/new potatoes
1 chicken stock cube
1 teaspoon salt, plus extra
  for seasoning
1 teaspoon Dijon mustard
freshly ground black pepper
100g crème fraîche
1–2 tablespoons grated Parmesan
  cheese (see tip on page 17)

GET AHEAD

• The recipe can be completed to the
  end of step 3 any time on the day,
  cooled, covered and set aside at
  room temperature, or up to a day
  in advance and kept in the fridge
  (bring back to room temperature an
  hour or so before cooking). Bake as
  above. If prepared in advance, the
  dish will take a little longer to cook
  in the oven.

This is an ideal recipe for entertaining as it can be prepared in advance and then finished off in the dish in which it's served. The recipe is easily doubled but use a larger shallow ovenproof dish which has a greater surface area, rather than a deeper one. The potatoes shouldn't be piled deeply. For vegetarians, use a vegetable stock cube and swap the Parmesan for a vegetarian Italian-style hard cheese.

1. Preheat the oven to 200°C/180°C fan/gas 6.

2. Slice each potato lengthways into three or four, depending on their size (no thicker than 1cm), put them into a large saucepan and barely cover with water. Crumble in the stock cube, add the measured salt and bring to the boil. Stir, then simmer for 8–10 minutes until the potatoes are just cooked. Drain the potatoes and tip them into a shallow, ovenproof dish.

3. Mix the mustard and a little salt and pepper into the crème fraîche and spoon this evenly over the hot potatoes. Scatter over the Parmesan.

4. Bake for 15–20 minutes until golden brown and bubbling. Serve.

Crisp Herby Potato Wedges

SERVES 4–6

500g medium-sized
  potatoes, unpeeled
salt
olive oil, for drizzling
sea salt flakes
large pinch of dried oregano
  or thyme

GET AHEAD

• Prepare to the end of step 3 any
  time on the day, then keep loosely
  covered at room temperature.
  When required, roast as above
  and serve.

• After roasting, the wedges will sit
  happily for an hour or so at room
  temperature. Leave them in the tin
  and reheat (temp as above) for
  5–10 minutes to crisp up again
  just before eating.

HINTS & TIPS

• It's important to use good-quality
  potatoes, named with their variety,
  such as Maris Piper or King Edward.

• Omit the par-cooking in step 2 if
  you're in a hurry and allow the
  potatoes a little longer in the oven.

So easy and tasty, these potatoes are good with many things, including barbecued food, steak, fish and chicken, or in their own right, dunked into a dip. Ring the changes by flavouring them with a sprinkling of spices, such as chilli, cumin, smoked paprika and different freshly chopped or dried herbs, before cooking. Suitable for vegetarians and vegans.

1. Preheat the oven to 220°C/200°C fan/gas 7.

2. Cut the potatoes in half lengthways and then cut each half into three or four wedges, depending on size. Add to a pan of cold well-salted water, bring to the boil and par-cook for 5 minutes. Drain and leave to steam dry for a few minutes.

3. Tip the potatoes into a shallow roasting tin or onto a baking tray large enough to take them all comfortably in one layer, drizzle over a little olive oil, sprinkle with some sea salt flakes and the oregano or thyme and gently mix so all the wedges are roughly coated. Don't worry if a few break up. Shake the tin to level and space them out into one layer.

4. Roast for 15–20 minutes, turning occasionally (don't turn until a crispy base has formed underneath and they lift willingly), until crisp and golden all over. Serve immediately.

Creamed Carrot & Cardamom Purée with Pine Nuts & Pumpkin Seeds

SERVES 4–5

500g carrots, peeled, halved
  and cut into even-sized chunks
2 green cardamom pods,
  cracked under the blade
  of a heavy knife
vegetable stock (or use chicken
  stock, if not vegetarian) – enough
  just to cover (or use 1 stock cube)
salt
good knob of butter, or more
  to taste
1 tablespoon crème fraîche,
  or more to taste
olive oil, for drizzling

For the topping
knob of butter
1 tablespoon pine nuts
1 tablespoon pumpkin seeds
freshly ground black pepper

Bright and colourful, healthy and inexpensive, vegetarian and fabulously get-ahead! The (optional) buttery topping adds a lovely bit of crunch. This is also good as a small plate or as part of a meze.

1. In a saucepan, barely cover the carrots and cardamom pods with stock, or cold water and a crumbled stock cube. Add some salt, bring to the boil and simmer until tender.

2. Meanwhile, make the topping. Melt the butter in a small frying pan or saucepan, add the pine nuts, pumpkin seeds and some black pepper and stir on a low-medium heat until the nuts are golden brown, about 3–5 minutes. Set aside in the pan.

3. Drain the carrots, fish out and discard the cardamom pods (although the inner seeds may be retained if you like) and leave the carrots to steam dry in the colander for a few minutes. Transfer them to a food-processor with the butter and whizz to a smooth purée. Add the crème fraîche and whizz again to incorporate. Taste and add more salt, butter and/or crème fraîche accordingly. It should be well seasoned.

4. To serve, spread out the purée in a shallow, open serving dish, making wavy ridges with the back of a spoon. Reheat the topping on a medium heat for 1–2 minutes until sizzling and then spoon into the middle of the purée. Grind some black pepper over the purée and finish with a swirl of olive oil. Serve.

GET AHEAD

• Make to the end of step 3 up to 3 days ahead and cool. Cover the purée and topping individually and chill. Alternatively, they can both be frozen (defrost before reheating). Reheat the purée (covered) in a preheated moderate oven (180°C/160°C fan/ gas 4) for 10–15 minutes until hot throughout, or microwave on High for 1–2 minutes until hot throughout, or stir in a pan on the stove in a little preheated oil or butter until hot. Reheat the topping as above (step 4).

HINTS & TIPS

• Alternative toppings for the purée include: toasted black sesame seeds; freshly chopped parsley or mint; parsley oil (parsley leaves and olive oil whizzed together to make a vibrant-green oil); a blob or swirl of thick Greek-style yoghurt or garlic-flavoured yoghurt; a swirl of pomegranate or date molasses; crumbled feta cheese and fresh pomegranate seeds (served with flatbreads for lunch or as a dip); grated hard cheese stirred into the purée until melted (very good with sausages!)

• The more butter and crème fraîche you add, the more luscious the purée becomes!

• Leave out the cardamom if you need a plainer, more traditional side dish as an accompaniment.

Celeriac with Peas, Mint & Cream

SERVES 6

30g butter
bunch of spring onions,
    trimmed and cut into
    roughly 3cm chunks
1 small celeriac (around 350g),
    peeled and cut into roughly
    1cm cubes
salt and freshly ground
    black pepper
1 x 28g vegetable (or chicken,
    if not vegetarian) stock pot
    (or use a vegetable/chicken
    stock cube)
350g frozen petit pois
3 tablespoons double cream
    (more if you like)
2 mint sprigs, leaves picked
    and roughly chopped

I love this recipe for when something with a sauce is required on the vegetable front. Fond as I am of veggies in a white sauce, sometimes that's a bit of an effort – enter this recipe with its simply created sauce, combining the tasty braising liquid with cream. Mint freshens it up and brings it all together.

Use this recipe just as a guide and incorporate other vegetable combos you might have to hand. It's a great prepare-ahead recipe when entertaining. Suitable for vegetarians.

1. Melt the butter in a sauté pan on a medium heat and when foaming, add the spring onions, celeriac and some seasoning. Cook on a gentle heat, turning over every so often, until the celeriac is soft but not coloured and still has a little bite, around 10 minutes. A little colour is fine though.

2. Still over the heat, push the celeriac aside to make a little space in the bottom of the pan; into this space add the stock pot (or crumbled stock cube) and 100ml of water and jiggle around to (almost) dissolve the stock pot (or stock cube). Stir in the frozen petit pois, bring to the boil, then reduce the heat and simmer gently for 5 minutes.

3. Stir in the cream and mint, heat through, check the seasoning and serve.

GET AHEAD

- Complete to the end of step 3 any time on the day, cool, cover and set aside in the pan at room temperature. Reheat gently on the stove until hot and just bubbling.

HINTS & TIPS

- Chicory, fennel, leeks and broad beans are good alternatives/ additions (keep overall quantities roughly the same).

- To transform the recipe into a vegetarian main course, add 1 x 400g tin of drained and rinsed chickpeas, flageolet beans or borlotti beans with the petit pois.

- Omit the cream altogether, or add more if you like.

- This is very good with cooked duck, grilled lamb chops or fish, or other grilled or fried food – in fact, pretty much anything.

Cauliflower Purée

SERVES 4

1 small-medium cauliflower,
  around 900g–1kg
salt
30g butter (more if you like),
  plus (optional) extra for
  frying cauli leaves
generous grating of nutmeg
1–2 tablespoons double cream
  or crème fraîche (optional)
olive oil, to serve (optional),
  plus (optional) extra for
  frying cauli leaves

A great vegetable side dish, made even better as it can be prepared in advance. The purée can be enhanced by whizzing in Parmesan or blue cheese, depending on what you're serving it with. It also makes a tasty base for fried scallops or baked or fried fish fillets. It's very good, too, as a small plate for lunch on its own, topped with toasted or fried nuts and seeds. Incorporating the cauliflower leaves gives the purée a lovely light green hue.

This is also ideal served with cooked steak, lamb or chicken and the Peppered Tuna Steaks (see page 87). We invariably eat this instead of potatoes. Suitable for vegetarians.

1. Discard any wilted, tough outer leaves from the cauliflower and reserve the remaining leaves (see also *Hints & Tips*). Snap or cut the florets into smallish, even-sized pieces and cut the inner fleshy part of the stem into small pieces.

2. Cook in a pan of boiling well-salted water, adding the leaves to the top of the pan, until tender, around 4–5 minutes. Drain well, allow the steam to subside for a few minutes, then tip into a food-processor. Add the butter and nutmeg, whizz to a smooth purée, then add and whizz in the cream or crème fraîche (if using). Check the seasoning (add more salt or nutmeg, if needed). It should be well-seasoned.

3. Transfer to a serving dish, drizzle with olive oil (if using) and serve, or keep the purée somewhere warm for 30 minutes or more before serving. If frying some of the reserved leaves as a topping (see *Hints & Tips*), fry them as directed, then arrange them atop the purée just before serving.

GET AHEAD

• Complete to the end of step 2 up to 3 days in advance, cool, cover and chill. Reheat in a saucepan (preferably non-stick) on a low heat, stirring, for a few minutes, until hot throughout. Alternatively, reheat in a covered ovenproof dish in a preheated moderate oven (180°C/160°C fan/gas 4) for 15 minutes; or reheat in a microwave on High for 1–2 minutes.

HINTS & TIPS

• I like to set aside a few inner cauliflower leaves and then fry them as a topping, which brings a lovely caramelised flavour to the purée. Simply fry the leaves in a little olive oil and butter for a few minutes until they begin to caramelise, then serve.

• For vegetarians, if using cheese (see intro), choose a vegetarian one, such as a vegetarian Italian-style hard cheese or Saint Agur.

Roast Parmesan Fennel

SERVES 4

olive oil, for greasing and drizzling
2 large (or 3 medium) fennel
   bulbs, tough outer layer and
   stems discarded (fronds reserved
   and roughly chopped) (optional)
¼ teaspoon fennel seeds,
   roughly crushed
salt and freshly ground
   black pepper
40g Parmesan cheese, grated
  (see tip on page 17)

GET AHEAD

• Complete to the end of step 2 any
time on the day. Cool, cover loosely
and leave at room temperature.
When cold, the Parmesan can
be sprinkled over the top. Reheat
in the oven (same temp as above)
for 5–8 minutes until hot throughout.

HINTS & TIPS

• Two large fennel bulbs yield 12
slices of fennel in total. Depending
on what else you're serving and the
size of the bulbs, you may like to
use three medium bulbs.

• Omit the Parmesan, if you prefer.

This is a very tasty way of serving fennel that can be cooked in advance and then finished off for a few minutes before serving. It's particularly good with anything grilled or fried such as steak, chops and fish. For vegetarians, swap the Parmesan for a vegetarian Italian-style hard cheese.

1. Preheat the oven to 220°C/200°C fan/gas 7. Lightly oil a (lipped) baking tray, no smaller than 37 x 27cm.

2. Halve the fennel bulbs through the root, then cut each half into three equal-sized slices, also through the root. Space the slices out on the oiled baking tray and scatter them with the fennel seeds and some seasoning, then drizzle with a little olive oil. Roast at the top of the oven for 12–15 minutes or until golden and caramelised on the underside. Turn the fennel over and roast for a further 5–6 minutes.

3. Sprinkle each slice with roughly 1 teaspoon of Parmesan, a little less over the smaller slices. Return to the oven for 5 minutes until the cheese is melted and bubbling. Arrange on a serving dish, scatter with the fennel fronds (if using) and serve.

Caramelised Soy Pak Choi

SERVES 4

4 pak choi (or 6, if small)
a glug of vegetable oil
a splash of sesame oil
1 tablespoon dark soy sauce
white and/or black sesame seeds,
toasted (optional) (see *Hints
& Tips* on page 40)

GET AHEAD

• Cook to the end of step 4 any time
on the day. Leave in the pan (loosely
covered) at room temperature, then
warm through on a gentle heat for a
few minutes when required. Or,
complete up to a day in advance,
cool, cover and chill. Reheat as
above, or arrange the pak choi in
one layer in a shallow roasting tin or
on a baking sheet, and reheat in a
moderate oven (180°C/160°C fan/
gas 4) for 5–8 minutes or until
heated through.

A lovely flavourful way of cooking pak choi, particularly when accompanying
Asian-style recipes; it also happens to look good! Perfect for entertaining
as all the cooking can be done in advance and reheating is all that's
necessary when required. Suitable for vegetarians and vegans.

1. Halve the pak choi lengthways through the root, and again into quarters
if any are large. Ensure the root is still intact and holding all the leaves
together.

2. Heat the vegetable and sesame oils in a large frying pan and add the pak
choi, cut-side down in one layer, head-to-tail, ensuring not to overcrowd
the pan too much (you may need to do this in several batches, depending
on the size of the pan and the pak choi).

3. Add a small splash of water and cook on a medium heat for around
5 minutes, until the water has evaporated, the pak choi is sizzling and
beginning to wilt and soften, and is caramelised underneath. Turn over
and cook for around 5 minutes more until a knife inserts through the root
easily, but the pak choi still has a bit of bite. If at any time you feel the
pak choi is browning too fast, simply add a splash of water and continue
cooking until it has evaporated.

4. Turn the pak choi cut-side down again, add the soy sauce and cook on
a low heat for a further minute or so until caramelised and a little charred.

5. Transfer the pak choi to a serving dish, cut-side up, sprinkle with toasted
sesame seeds (if using) and serve.

Fried Chicory with Walnuts

SERVES 4

2 heads of chicory
good glug of olive oil
generous knob of butter
salt and freshly ground
  black pepper
40g walnut pieces

GET AHEAD

• Complete to the end of step 2 any
  time on the day and leave in the
  pan (loosely covered) at room
  temperature. Warm through on a
  gentle heat for 5–10 minutes until
  hot throughout, when required.
  Or, complete up to a day in
  advance, cool, cover and chill.
  Transfer to the pan to reheat as
  above. Finish the recipe (step 3)
  as above.

HINTS & TIPS

• Omit the walnuts, if you prefer.

• If you're after a bit of colour for the
  final dish, scatter with a little freshly
  chopped parsley.

Chicory just happens to be one of my favourite things to eat, raw or cooked, in equal measure. This is such a quick way of cooking chicory, transforming it into a lovely accompaniment, in particular for steak, beef, duck breasts and fish. Suitable for vegetarians.

1. Remove any wilted or damaged outside leaves from the chicory and slice the thinnest sliver off the root, making sure all the leaves are still attached. Cut each head in half through the root.

2. Heat the olive oil and butter in a heavy, lidded sauté pan, into which the chicory will fit fairly snugly. When the butter is foaming, sprinkle the base of the pan with a little salt and add the chicory halves, cut-side down, head-to-tail. Season, cover with the lid and cook on a very low heat for 10 minutes. Turn the chicory over, replace the lid and cook for a further 5 minutes. If at any time during cooking, the chicory is browning too fast or the butter looks like burning (this will depend on the water content of the chicory), just add a splash of cold water and continue cooking until it has evaporated.

3. Transfer the chicory to a serving dish, cut-side up and keep warm. Assuming the butter isn't too dark (if it is, discard it, wipe out the pan and melt a generous knob of fresh butter), add the walnuts to the pan and cook on a medium heat for 1–2 minutes, scraping and stirring, until they're coated in the delicious sticky pan juices. Spoon the walnuts over the chicory and serve.

Tomato & Chilli Salad

SERVES 4

300g ripe, best-quality mixed
   tomatoes
sea salt flakes and freshly
   ground black pepper
dried chilli flakes, to taste
extra-virgin olive oil, for drizzling

To garnish
fresh chive flowers and/or
   wild garlic flowers, torn apart;
   basil leaves; snipped salad cress

GET AHEAD

• Step 1 can be completed any time
   on the day, covered and left at room
   temperature. Before continuing with
   step 2, if necessary soak up any
   excess liquid from the tomatoes with
   kitchen paper.

HINTS & TIPS

• Ring the changes by swapping the
   olive oil for avocado or basil oil.

• Top the salad with a few spring
   onions, trimmed and thinly sliced
   diagonally, or shaved raw fennel,
   if you like.

So often, the simplest things are best, and this 'recipe' is a case in point.
The chilli offers a kick that takes everyone by surprise, and it goes without
saying that the best tomatoes, and olive oil, too, are vital. Choose heritage
tomatoes if you can and in as many different sizes, shapes and colours as
you like. Suitable for vegetarians and vegans.

1. Slice the tomatoes, with a serrated-edge knife, according to their size.
I like to thinly slice larger tomatoes and halve or quarter smaller baby plum
or cherry tomatoes, depending on their size. Arrange prettily on a platter.

2. Just before serving, season the tomatoes with salt and pepper and scatter
with a few chilli flakes, according to your taste. Drizzle with olive oil and
finish with the garnish(es) of your choice.

Platters & Picnics

Platters are, without doubt, my favourite way of presenting and serving food. They look bountiful, generous and appealing. It's very enticing seeing all the components on show, just willing you to get stuck in. To me, platters shout feast and sharing, and a beautifully arranged platter can turn even the simplest ingredients into a stunning centrepiece and something special.

Warm Roasted Spiced Cauliflower with Butternut Squash & Maftoul

SERVES 6 as a main course
(or serves more as part of
a buffet, with other salads)

olive oil, for greasing and drizzling
1 small cauliflower, about 700–750g
1 butternut squash, about 650g,
   peeled, halved and de-seeded
125g giant white couscous
   (aka maftoul or moghrabieh)
salt

For the spice mix
½ teaspoon garam masala
½ teaspoon ground sumac
½ teaspoon ground turmeric
½ teaspoon each black and
   white mustard seeds
1 teaspoon salt
½ teaspoon cracked or freshly
   ground black pepper
4 tablespoons olive oil

For the dressing
juice of ½ lemon
¼ teaspoon salt
½ tablespoon ground sumac

GET AHEAD

• The recipe can be completed up to
  2 days in advance (but don't dress
  the salad until just before serving),
  covered and stored in the fridge.
  Bring back to room temperature, or
  reheat in the tin in a preheated oven
  at 200°C/180°C fan/gas 6 for
  10–12 minutes until hot throughout,
  before serving.

Spicy and lemony, this vegetarian and vegan salad is as good served warm as it is at room temperature. The recipe calls for white maftoul (giant couscous) but do use wholewheat couscous, if you prefer. The spice list makes the recipe seem lengthy, but these are mainly store cupboard ingredients, and the vegetables are roasted together in one pan – so don't be put off! This makes a delicious side dish as well, served warm or at room temperature

1. Preheat the oven to 220°C/200°C fan/gas 7. Find a shallow roasting tin or a large (lipped) baking tray around 41 x 26 x 4cm and grease it very lightly with a smear of olive oil.

2. Discard the tough outer leaves from the cauliflower, then cut off and reserve the fresh inner leaves, halving any bigger ones lengthways through the stem. Snap off or cut the head into even-sized, but not too big, florets. Cut off and discard the tough outer edges of the core/stem, and cut the remaining inner fleshy part into bite-sized pieces. Put the florets, leaves and inner stem pieces into the prepared tin. Cut the butternut squash into chunks smaller than the florets and add to the tin.

3. Combine all the spice mix ingredients together in a small bowl, pour over the vegetables and mix well to coat everything, then drizzle with a little extra olive oil. Roast at the top of the oven for 20–25 minutes or until the vegetables are just tender and a little charred in places.

4. Meanwhile, cook the couscous in a medium pan of boiling well-salted water for 6 minutes. Drain well in a sieve. I like to dry the couscous further in a bowl lined with kitchen paper, although it does stick to the paper a bit, but it's easily peeled off. A little olive oil helps to keep the grains separate. Mix the dressing ingredients together in a small bowl.

5. Tip the couscous over the vegetables in the tin while they're still warm and gently combine them. Arrange the salad on a platter, ensuring some of the lovely charred leaves are on top as a garnish. Spoon the dressing over the salad, finish with a swirl of olive oil and serve.

• The dressing and spice mix can be
  made (separately) up to 2 days in
  advance. Cover and keep at room
  temperature.

HINTS & TIPS

• Wholewheat couscous will take
  a little longer to cook.

Prawn, Avocado & Mango Salad

SERVES 5–6
(or serves 8 generously
as a starter)

2 perfectly ripe mangoes,
  peeled and cut into long slivers
  (see *Hints & Tips*)
500g frozen cooked, peeled
  jumbo king prawns, defrosted,
  rinsed and patted dry on
  kitchen paper
1 mild red chilli, de-seeded and
  finely chopped
a bunch of coriander (around
  30g), roughly chopped
2 ripe avocados
around 70g rocket leaves,
  to serve

For the dressing
juice of 1 lime
6 tablespoons (90ml) walnut
  or avocado oil
½ teaspoon light soft brown,
  palm or light muscovado sugar
salt and freshly ground
  black pepper

Wonderfully refreshing and bursting with very tasty juices, the quality of this salad depends entirely on the ripeness of the mangoes and the flavour of the prawns. I have my good friend (and good cook and recipe tester) Amanda to thank for this recipe. She says it's been one of her standbys for years, and with very good reason. I can remember the flavours from the first time I had it as though it were yesterday. It's very good as a starter, too.

1. Put the mango slivers into a large mixing bowl with the prawns, chilli and coriander. Cut the avocados in half, remove the stones and cut into long thin slices within their skins, using a round-bladed knife. Scoop the flesh out into the bowl using a tablespoon.

2. Whisk the dressing ingredients together in a small bowl, seasoning well with salt and pepper.

3. Just before serving, spoon the dressing over the salad, holding a little back as you may not need it all, and very gently combine everything in the bowl. Scatter the rocket leaves over a large platter or shallow open bowl and arrange the salad on top. Serve immediately.

GET AHEAD

- The mangoes, chilli and coriander can be prepared any time on the day (chill the prepped mango), and step 1 can be completed up to an hour in advance.

- Step 2 can be completed up to 2 days in advance, covered and chilled.

HINTS & TIPS

- To prepare the mangoes, slice the flesh from either side of the flat, oval stone. Using a round-bladed knife, slice the flesh within (and without piercing) its skin into finger-sized slices, then scoop the slices out with a tablespoon, being careful not to leave any flesh behind in the skin. Peel the skin from the remaining flesh on the side of the mango stone and slice into strips.

- If time is short, use a packet(s) of ready-prepared sliced fresh ripe mango.

- Serve on individual plates as a starter or light lunch, if you prefer.

- This recipe is easily halved.

Hot & Cold Smoked Salmon, New Potato & Asparagus Salad with Lemon, Dill & Horseradish Sauce

SERVES 6–8

750g waxy new/salad potatoes
salt and freshly ground black pepper
250g asparagus (more if you like),
  woody ends snapped off and
  discarded
1 fennel bulb, tough outer layer
  and stems removed and discarded,
  ferny fronds chopped
85g watercress
300g hot-smoked salmon fillets,
  skinned and flaked (or use a
  packet(s) of ready-flaked)
4 spring onions, trimmed and
  thinly sliced diagonally
100g thinly sliced smoked salmon,
  snipped into fat ribbons
15–20g dill, chopped

For the sauce
100g crème fraîche
5 teaspoons creamed hot
  horseradish sauce
1 teaspoon Dijon mustard
juice of 1 large lemon

GET AHEAD

• The salad can be put together entirely,
any time on the day. Surprisingly it
doesn't go at all soggy, which makes
it great for picnics. Keep the salad
loosely covered at room temperature,
unless prepping a good few hours
in advance, in which case, chill in
the fridge and bring back to room
temperature to serve.

This colourful, pretty salad is made with easy-to-pick-up ingredients and is so simple to put together. Great for picnics, as it can be completed well in advance, it's really just an assembly job, which is a gift particularly on a hot day. Based on Scandi flavours, it's fresh and crunchy, lemony and piquant – and extremely tasty. Ensure all the components are visible in the finished extravaganza!

1. Bring the potatoes to the boil in a pan of very well-salted water and simmer until just tender. Drain, and when cool enough to handle and depending on their size, cut each into three or more chunky wedges (no smaller than a whole walnut), or just halve, if small. Set aside to cool.

2. Cook the asparagus in a pan of boiling very well-salted water for a few minutes, until just tender. Drain, immediately cool under cold water, then roll up in kitchen paper to dry. Set aside.

3. Mix all the sauce ingredients, except the lemon juice, together in a bowl, adding salt and pepper to taste, then gradually add 2–3 tablespoons of the lemon juice to taste. The sauce should be very highly seasoned. You may not need all the lemon juice or you may choose to loosen the sauce further with a little more lemon juice or some cold water.

4. Cut the fennel bulb in half through the root, then shave across into thin slices with a mandolin or by hand. Set aside.

5. To assemble the salad, spread the potatoes out over the bottom of a large, oval platter (approx. 48 x 35cm or a comparable round size) and season. Nestle the watercress into the potatoes, snapping any large stems in two. Scatter with the fennel, then the hot-smoked salmon. Halve the asparagus spears (or cut into thirds if very long) and arrange over the fennel, followed by half the spring onions. Spoon over the sauce, then drape the smoked salmon ribbons over the top. Scatter with the remaining spring onions; the fennel fronds and dill, then serve.

HINTS & TIPS

• Step 1 and step 3 can be completed, and the spring onions can be prepared, up to 3 days ahead. Keep covered in the fridge.

• If the new potatoes aren't the tastiest, inject some flavour by spooning 2 tablespoons of French dressing over them, after cutting into chunks and while they're still warm.

Russian-style Runner Bean Salad

SERVES 4–5 as a main course
(or serves more as part of a
selection of salads)

250g waxy new/salad potatoes
salt and freshly ground
  black pepper
450g runner beans, topped,
  tailed, strings removed,
  then very thinly sliced
2 eggs, boiled for 7 minutes,
  cooled, peeled and cut into
  rough chunks
10 cocktail gherkins, drained
  and chunkily sliced
2 tablespoons small capers
  in brine, drained
6 tablespoons thick mayonnaise
  (see notes on page 17)
180–200g cooked ham, diced,
  or shredded ham hock
20g dill, 2 sprigs reserved,
  thick bottom stems removed
  and the remainder roughly
  chopped
salad leaves, to finish (optional)

We grow a lot of runner beans and at their peak we are inundated. This
(as well as in white sauce) is a favourite way of preparing them. Roughly
based on ingredients for a Russian salad, it's extremely flavourful. For the
best possible success, do get the beans as dry as possible before adding the
other ingredients.

I use a handy runner bean slicer for preparing the beans, which has an
integral blade for topping and tailing, and it strings and slices in one go;
they then need cutting to your preferred length.

1. Bring the potatoes to the boil in a pan of well-salted water and cook
until just tender. Drain, cool and cut into bite-sized chunks. Put into a
large mixing bowl.

2. Cook the beans in a pan of boiling well-salted water for 2 minutes,
drain and run under cold water in a colander until cool. They should be
bright green. Tap hard to remove the excess water, then spread them out
on kitchen paper, cover with more kitchen paper and roll up to dry the
beans. Leave for a few minutes to absorb the water. When dry, add them
to the mixing bowl, followed by all the remaining ingredients (except the
reserved dill sprigs and salad leaves).

3. Using a large spoon, very lightly and gently combine the ingredients.
The aim is to keep everything chunky and fresh, rather than to end up
with a mayonnaise-y mush. The vegetables should only be lightly coated
in mayonnaise and not at all watery. Check the seasoning: the salad should
be very well seasoned.

4. Spoon the salad onto a serving platter, garnish with the dill sprigs and
finish with some salad leaves (if using).

GET AHEAD

• All the components of the salad,
  except for the dill, can be prepared
  up to 2 days in advance and stored
  separately, covered and chilled.
  Bring back to room temperature
  before serving.

HINTS & TIPS

• Use the recipe as a guide only
  and adjust quantities up or down,
  according to what you have to
  hand. This is a good way of using
  up leftover potatoes and ham, not to
  mention a glut of runner beans.

• Hard-boiled eggs keep well, peeled
  and submerged in a bowl of cold
  water, covered and chilled. They
  will keep for several days like this.
  The water prevents them from going
  rubbery.

Chorizo, Red Pepper & Cheddar Picnic Tartlets

MAKES 12

butter, for greasing
plain flour, for dusting
½ x 320g chilled ready-rolled
   shortcrust pastry sheet (freeze
   the unused half sheet, or see
   Hints & Tips)
5cm piece of spicy chorizo,
   skinned and cut into ½cm dice
30g roasted red peppers from a jar,
   drained and cut into ½cm dice
1 egg, plus 1 egg yolk
30g mature Cheddar cheese, grated
pinch of dried oregano
50ml double cream (or use
   50g crème fraîche)
salt and freshly ground
   black pepper

These are simple rustic little tarts that pack a huge flavour punch for their size. Very inexpensive to make, they're light and moreish – in fact, you might like to make a double batch as they're pop-in-the-mouth good!

1. Preheat the oven to 200°C/180°C fan/gas 6. Lightly butter a 12-hole mince pie tin (with round-bottomed holes).

2. On a lightly floured worktop, roll out the pastry to about 1mm thick, and stamp out 12 discs using an 8cm plain cutter. Line the buttered tin with the discs. You may need to stack up and re-roll the offcuts for the last 2–3 discs.

3. Divide the chorizo and red pepper between the pastry cases. In a jug, whisk the egg and egg yolk together with a fork, then mix in the cheese, oregano, cream (or crème fraîche) and some seasoning.

4. Spoon into the pastry cases, dividing the custard equally between them. Bake for 12–15 minutes until just set. Cool in the tin for 5–10 minutes before serving or transferring to a wire rack to cool completely. Serve warm or at room temperature.

GET AHEAD

- The recipe can be completed up to 3 days in advance, cooled, covered and chilled. Serve at room temperature, or reheat in the oven (temp as above) for a few minutes until warm.

- Steps 2 and 3 can be completed up to 2 days in advance and stored separately, covered and chilled.

- The tartlets can also be frozen. Defrost before reheating (as above) to freshen them up (I wouldn't advise eating them after defrosting without having reheated them, to dispel the freezer 'taste'; they can be eaten cold thereafter).

HINTS & TIPS

- To save time for a later date, cut discs out of the unused half pastry sheet and freeze these, interleaved with clingfilm or baking parchment (For this, re-use the baking parchment the pastry is rolled in, cut into squares). Alternatively, make a double batch of tartlets and freeze one batch.

- The leftover pastry trimmings can be gathered together and re-rolled (once) to produce more discs.

Cheat's Coronation Chicken

SERVES 6

1 whole cooked chicken
(900–950g cooked weight), or
poach your own (see *Hints & Tips*)
250g best-quality thick mayonnaise
(see notes on page 17)
2–2½ teaspoons curry paste,
depending on the paste
and your taste
2 tablespoons mango chutney
salt and freshly ground
black pepper
2 tablespoons toasted flaked
almonds
watercress sprigs, to garnish

GET AHEAD

- Complete to the end of step 3 up to
2 days in advance, cover and chill.
Bring back to room temperature
before serving.

HINTS & TIPS

- A whole 1.3–1.5kg (raw weight)
chicken (950g–1kg whole cooked
weight) yields around 500g of meat.

- To poach a whole chicken, place
the whole oven-ready chicken
(about 1.3–1.5kg) in a saucepan
into which it fits fairly snugly. Barely
cover it with water, add a quartered
onion, 2 bay leaves, a few black

Surely one of the best and most enduring recipes of all time, and with
good reason, developed to celebrate the coronation of Queen Elizabeth II.
I wouldn't assume to tamper with it for improvement but merely, in this
case, to simplify and make the recipe quicker. Curry powder needs to be
cooked to bring out its flavour, whereas curry paste doesn't, so, using the
latter cuts out a stage in the original recipe.

If you use a top-quality ready-cooked chicken, there is no actual cooking
involved. Home-made mayonnaise is preferable as the flavour works much
better, but ready-made is fine as long as it is also the best quality.

Serve with cold rice – I like using pre-mixed (uncooked) Basmati and
wild rice, and we absolutely love this with the Tomato & Chilli Salad
(see page 167).

1. Remove the skin and bones from the chicken and discard, then tear or
shred the meat into pieces and put into a large bowl.

2. In a small bowl, whisk together the mayonnaise, curry paste and chutney
(if using thick home-made mayonnaise, the sauce may need loosening to a
smooth coating consistency by whisking in a little warm water). Pour the
mayonnaise, holding back 1 tablespoon, over the chicken and gently mix
everything together with a large spoon. Don't over-mix otherwise the
chicken will become shredded. Taste and season accordingly.

3. Arrange the chicken on a serving platter. Whisk a little warm water into
the reserved mayonnaise until it's just thin enough to lightly coat the back
of a spoon. Spoon this over the top of the chicken.

4. Scatter with the flaked almonds and garnish with sprigs of watercress.

peppercorns and any other
aromatics you like. Cover, bring to
the boil, then reduce the heat and
simmer gently for 1 hour or until
cooked through. Remove the pan
from the heat and leave the chicken
to cool completely in its liquid.
When cool, drain the chicken (retain
the stock for another use), then skin,
de-bone, and shred the meat.

- Boiled new potatoes or nutty
Camargue red rice are alternative
accompaniments, as is a leafy green
salad. The chicken is very rich so
keep the accompaniments as plain
as possible.

- Add a little lime pickle (from a jar)
to the mayonnaise if you like a little
more heat.

Tomato, Taleggio & Basil Tart

SERVES 4–6
(or serves 8 as part of a buffet)

1 x 320g chilled ready-rolled
  shortcrust pastry sheet
plain flour, for dusting
3–4 large or 5–6 medium tomatoes,
  thinly sliced through the 'equator',
  both ends discarded (a serrated
  knife is easiest for this)
dried chilli flakes, to taste (optional)
sea salt flakes and freshly
  ground black pepper
200g Taleggio cheese, thinly sliced,
  including the rind
1 basil sprig, leaves picked
olive oil, for drizzling

A simple rustic tart bursting with summer flavours, this is great for pulling out of the hat at short notice. Particularly good for when tomatoes are at their best. For vegetarians, either choose a creamy vegetarian cheese or leave out the cheese altogether.

1. Preheat the oven to 200°C/180°C fan/gas 6.

2. Unroll the pastry, peel it off its baking parchment wrapping paper, dust the paper with a little flour, then replace the pastry and slide it, on its paper, onto a baking sheet. Prick well all over with a fork. Bake for 12–15 minutes or until a lightly golden biscuit colour (cover the corners with the paper partway through baking if they're browning too quickly).

3. Arrange the tomatoes, slightly overlapping, down the length of the pastry in three or four columns (depending on the size of the tomatoes), leaving a slight margin around the edges. Scatter with a few chilli flakes (if using) and season generously with salt and pepper. Break up the sliced cheese and dot over the tomatoes. Season again, scatter over the basil leaves, tearing any larger ones, then drizzle with a little olive oil.

4. Bake for 15–20 minutes until the cheese is molten (if using) and just beginning to brown. Serve warm or at room temperature, cut into pieces the size of your choice, trimming the edges first if necessary. Slide the tart onto a board, with or without its baking parchment, and drizzle with olive oil just before serving.

GET AHEAD

- Step 2 can be completed up to 3 days in advance, cooled, covered and kept somewhere cool. It can also be frozen (defrost before continuing).

- The tomatoes can be sliced hours in advance and kept at room temperature. Discard any leaked juices.

- The whole tart can be cooked in advance on the day and kept/ served at room temperature, or warmed up in the oven (temp as above) for a few minutes just before required.

HINTS & TIPS

- Swap the basil for thyme, oregano, marjoram, summer savory or chives.

- Snipped salad cress or micro leaves are also good alternatives to the final scattering of basil, as are chive flowers, broken up into petals.

- Swap the sea salt flakes for smoked sea salt flakes.

Portable Prawn Cocktail

SERVES 4

1½ Little Gem lettuces, very,
   very thinly sliced or shredded
5cm piece of cucumber, cut into
   ½cm dice (optional)
240g cooked, peeled prawns
   (if using frozen, approx. 300g
   frozen weight), defrosted (if
   frozen), rinsed and patted dry
   on kitchen paper
paprika (regular, smoked or
   hot smoked), for dusting
½ lime, cut into 4 wedges

For the cocktail sauce
5 tablespoons thick mayonnaise
   (see notes on page 17)
1½ tablespoons tomato ketchup
4–6 drops of Worcestershire sauce
   (more if you like)
6 drops of Tabasco sauce
   (more if you like)

I have been making individual little picnic pots of prawn cocktail for years, simply because they're so popular and always received with delight. Often the highlight of a picnic, perhaps it's having one's own individual serving, or simply universal devotion to prawn cocktail, or both! I recycle jam jars and small containers/pots with lids from supermarket purchases, which I keep for this purpose. See *Hints & Tips* below for picnic pot details. Of course, the recipe can be made in glasses for eating at home, in which case you might like to add a little diced avocado and a cooked shell-on prawn to each glass for garnish.

1. Divide the shredded lettuce between 4 x 250g/ml capacity pots with lids. Top with the cucumber (if using) and then the prawns. Lightly press everything down a little.

2. Mix together all the sauce ingredients in a bowl, taste, and if necessary, adjust according to your taste. It should have a bit of a kick to it. If the sauce is very thick, you may need to loosen it a tad to a coating consistency with a little warm water (although it shouldn't in any way be runny – this will depend on the texture of the mayonnaise at the outset).

3. Spoon the sauce over the prawns, dust with paprika and garnish each serving with a wedge of lime to the side. Cover with the lids and keep in the fridge. When packing up the picnic, don't forget the teaspoons!

GET AHEAD

• The recipe can be made entirely up to 2 days in advance and kept in the fridge. The sauce can be made up to a week in advance, covered and chilled.

HINTS & TIPS

• Aim for plain jars and pots without lettering on them – the ones enclosed in a cardboard sleeve are usually plain underneath. Pots for ricotta and mascarpone cheese or for dips such as hummus and so on, are just the job. Small Kilner-style jars work well, too. Remember that plastic supermarket pots are lighter to transport than jam jars!

Duck Breast Salad with Vietnamese-style Dressing

SERVES 6 (generously)

4 duck breasts, about 150–160g
   each, trimmed, skin-on
½ teaspoon Chinese
   five-spice powder
salt
½ small red onion, very finely
   sliced (with a mandolin,
   if you have one)
30g coriander, roughly chopped
20g mint, leaves picked and
   roughly chopped
85g salted or dry roasted peanuts,
   roughly chopped
500g chilled fresh ready-to-eat
   egg noodles
40g (2 tablespoons) fresh
   pomegranate seeds
good pinch of toasted sesame
   seeds (see *Hints & Tips* on
   page 40), for sprinkling

For the dressing
1 large mild red chilli, halved,
   de-seeded and finely chopped
1 teaspoon ginger purée
   from a jar or tube
1 teaspoon light muscovado
   or light soft brown sugar
2½ tablespoons fish sauce
juice of 1 lime
2 tablespoons vegetable oil
1 tablespoon toasted sesame oil

Meltingly tender, juicy duck breasts and a fresh, flavourful herby dressing make this a winning and popular main course salad. It's very easy, too.

1. Preheat the oven to 220°C/200°C fan/gas 7.

2. Score the skin of the duck breasts in a criss-cross pattern with the point of a sharp knife. Rub the skin with the five-spice powder and a little salt.

3. Heat a dry, ovenproof (preferably) frying pan and when smoking hot, cook the duck breasts, skin-side down, on a medium heat for 5 minutes until brown and crisp. Turn over, transfer the pan to the oven (or transfer the breasts, skin-side up, to a small, shallow roasting tin) and roast for 6 minutes. Remove the breasts to a plate immediately and leave to cool.

4. While the duck is cooking, mix the dressing ingredients together in a small bowl and set aside.

5. Cut the duck breasts into slices (reserve any resting juices) roughly ½cm thick, then cut each slice vertically into two or three bite-sized pieces, depending on the size of the slice. Put into a large bowl with the onion, coriander, mint and all but 1 tablespoon of the peanuts. Add any duck resting juices to the dressing, then pour this over the salad and very gently mix everything together.

6. Spread the noodles over a serving platter and arrange the duck salad over the top, leaving a margin of noodles visible around the edge. Scatter the pomegranate seeds over the top and then gently nestle the duck mixture into the noodles. Scatter with the toasted sesame seeds and the reserved peanuts and serve immediately.

GET AHEAD

- Steps 2, 3 and 4 can be completed up to 2 days in advance. Cool the duck, cover and chill. Cover and chill the dressing. Bring both back to room temperature before serving.

HINTS & TIPS

- Scatter a couple of handfuls of cos, Little Gem or other substantial lettuce leaves over the base of the serving platter, before adding the noodles and duck salad, if you like.

Burrata, Radicchio & Candied Walnuts with Sourdough Crisps

SERVES 4–5

3 very thin slices sourdough,
  or other artisan bread
olive oil, for drizzling
sea salt flakes
75g walnut halves
2 tablespoons clear honey
150g round head of radicchio,
  separated into leaves, or other
  mixed bitter leaves
2 handfuls of rocket leaves
2 burrata cheeses, drained
micro leaves or salad cress,
  to finish (optional)

For the dressing
2 teaspoons Dijon mustard
2 teaspoons sherry vinegar
scant ½ teaspoon salt
freshly ground black pepper,
  to taste
3 tablespoons olive oil
3 tablespoons walnut oil

GET AHEAD

• Steps 2 and 3 can be completed
up to 3 days in advance and stored
in separate airtight containers,
although they will both last a lot
longer.

• The dressing can be made up
to 3 days in advance, covered
and chilled.

Fresh, colourful, bitter leaves contrast with brittle, sweet, candied walnuts and delicate creamy burrata in this very tempting platter. The crisps are very moreish (be warned!) and can be made with any artisan bread – it's worth making extra, as they keep in an airtight container for several weeks and can also be frozen. They're handy for scattering on other salads, too, or (snapped into smaller pieces) as canapé bases. For vegetarians, ensure the burratas you use are suitable.

1. Preheat the oven to 200°C/180°C fan/gas 6.

2. Put the slices of bread onto a baking sheet, drizzle with a little olive oil, scatter with salt and bake for 8–10 minutes (watch them!) until crisp and dried out. Transfer to a wire rack. They will crisp up further as they cool.

3. Line a plate with baking parchment or silicone paper and set aside. Put the walnuts and honey into a small frying pan and cook on a medium heat for 4–5 minutes, stirring, until the nuts caramelise and turn deep golden brown (when the nuts begin to smoke is a good indication of when they're ready). Quickly tip the nuts out of the pan onto the parchment or paper, spread them out and leave to cool.

4. Mix all the dressing ingredients together in a small bowl, adding ½ tablespoon of cold water and whisking until they form a thick emulsion. This may take a minute or two.

5. Arrange the radicchio and rocket leaves on a platter. Dot the burrata over the top, breaking it up into chunky bite-sized pieces, and then spoon over the dressing. Scatter over the candied walnuts. Snap the sourdough crisps into bite-sized pieces, scatter over the top of the salad, followed by the micro leaves or salad cress (if using), and serve.

HINTS & TIPS

• Candied walnuts are a very good addition to a cheeseboard. And, resembling sugar-coated sweets as they do, piled into a small pretty bowl and handed round after dinner, they are always popular.

• The easy way of removing caramel from a pan is to fill it with water and bring it to the boil, popping any sticky utensils in there, too.

Chopped Salad with Feta Cheese & Cannellini Beans

SERVES 4–6 as a main course
(or serves more as a side or as
part of a buffet)

½ cucumber, cut into 1cm dice
1 small red pepper, de-seeded
    and cut into 1cm dice
2 celery sticks, stringy bits removed
    with a peeler, cut into 1cm dice
1 small fennel bulb, tough
    outer layer and stems discarded,
    cut into 1cm dice
4 spring onions, trimmed and
    thinly sliced diagonally
20 (small) cherry tomatoes,
    quartered
200g feta cheese (bearing the
    PDO logo), cut into 1cm dice
1 x 400g tin cannellini beans,
    drained, rinsed and dried
    on kitchen paper
4 tablespoons olive oil
1½ tablespoons pomegranate
    molasses
good pinch of dried oregano
25g mint, leaves picked
    and chopped
salt and freshly ground
    black pepper

Crunchy, refreshing and healthy best sums up a chopped salad. Traditionally, all the ingredients are cut to the same size, plus here I have added feta cheese and cannellini beans, transforming it into a main course. That said, this makes a great accompaniment to a buffet, alongside other salads. If you have vegetarian guests, ensure the feta you use is suitable. Omit the feta and beans and it's a lovely accompaniment to almost anything, which also happens to be vegetarian and vegan.

1. Mix all the vegetables, the feta and cannellini beans together in a large bowl.

2. Add all the remaining ingredients, stir to combine and season generously. Arrange on/in a shallow platter (rather than a deep bowl), and serve.

GET AHEAD

- Step 1 can be completed any time on the day (keep the tomatoes separate, and discard any leaked juices before adding them to the other ingredients), covered and set aside at room temperature. Dress the salad just before serving.

HINTS & TIPS

- A tablespoon of ground sumac added with the dressing ingredients offers a lovely lemony kick.

- Swap the feta for fried diced halloumi (or fried slices), arranging them over the top of the salad.

- Be relaxed about the ingredients and leave out anything you haven't got or don't like, or include others such as diced raw courgettes.

Leeks Vinaigrette

SERVES 4 as a main course
salad (or serves 8 as a starter
or 4 as a small plate)

4 small-medium leeks, uniform in
  size, around 2.5cm thick (no more)
salt and freshly ground black pepper
2 eggs, boiled for 7 minutes,
  cooled, peeled and chopped
  (see *Hints & Tips*)
1 tablespoon finely chopped shallot
  (around ½ shallot), or 1 spring
  onion, trimmed and chopped
20g walnut pieces, toasted
  and roughly chopped (see *Hints
  & Tips* on page 97)
2 tablespoons snipped chives
2 tarragon sprigs, leaves picked
  and chopped, or ½ teaspoon
  dried tarragon
4 anchovy fillets in oil, drained
  and snipped into slivers
1 heaped teaspoon small capers
  in brine, drained
a few tarragon leaves and/or
  whole chives (optional)

For the dressing
1 tablespoon Dijon mustard
½ tablespoon red wine vinegar
1 teaspoon water
¼ teaspoon salt
4 tablespoons olive oil
1 tablespoon walnut oil

Simple, pretty, utterly delicious, and a classic! As well as being a really great get-ahead dish, it's an economical one, too. Arranged on platters, the leeks are lovely for large parties as well. I was undecided in which chapter to include this recipe, it being so versatile – starter, small plate, lunch, supper, side salad…

For a speedier version, the dressed leeks are just as good without the herby egg topping. The smaller the leeks, the better.

1. Discard the tough outer leaves from the leeks and trim any root fibres, leaving the root intact and all the leaves still attached. Slice off and discard the tough dark green leaves from the top of each leek, forming a point by making two diagonal cuts (the leeks should all be the same length). Split them lengthways, about 5cm from the top, and rinse under the tap, flicking as if through the pages of a book, to remove any soil.

2. Lay the leeks flat in a large sauté or frying pan, shallow casserole or roasting tin, add two generous pinches of salt and pour over enough boiling water from the kettle just to cover them. Simmer gently for around 7–8 minutes, until the root is tender when pierced with the point of a knife. Drain, plunge the leeks into cold water and leave until cold. Drain upside-down and then gently squeeze the tips of the leeks to extract any water. Carefully roll up in kitchen paper to soak up the excess water.

3. Meanwhile, put all the dressing ingredients into a small bowl and whisk together until they form a thick emulsion (which might take a minute or two).

4. Put the chopped eggs, shallot or spring onion, walnuts and snipped/chopped (or dried) herbs into a small bowl with some seasoning and gently combine everything, being very careful not to over-mix as the egg yolk will disintegrate.

5. Cut the leeks in half lengthways, arrange cut-side up on a pretty platter (uniformly or nose-to-tail), sprinkle with a little salt and drizzle over all but a spoonful of the dressing, leaving the leeks dressing-free and visible at either end. Scatter over the egg mixture (again, leaving the leek ends visible) and then spoon over the last of the dressing. Finish with the anchovies, capers and tarragon leaves and/or whole chives (if using), and serve.

GET AHEAD

• Complete steps 1, 2 and 3 up to 3
  days in advance; wrap the leeks (in
  the kitchen paper) in clingfilm and
  chill. Cover and chill the dressing.

• Prepare step 4 any time on the day,
  but don't combine until required.
  Keep loosely covered at room
  temperature.

HINTS & TIPS

• The easiest way to chop an egg is
  to use an egg slicer – cut into slices
  the usual way, then turn the egg
  90 degrees, slice again and tip the
  resulting dice into a bowl.

Warm Honey-roasted Figs with Parma Ham, Feta, Rocket & Pesto Sauce

SERVES 4

1–2 tablespoons olive oil, plus extra for greasing and drizzling
4 ripe figs, cut into quarters through the stem, or halved if small
3 teaspoons clear honey
70–80g rocket leaves
150g feta cheese (bearing the PDO logo)
sea salt flakes and freshly ground black pepper
1–2 tablespoons good-quality pesto sauce (see notes on page 17)
6 slices Parma ham, halved widthways and rolled into cigarette shapes
1 tablespoon pine nuts, toasted

A fresh, light and flavourful main course (or leave out the Parma ham for a tasty side salad) that is more of an assembly job than a recipe. Ensure you use the best quality feta cheese that bears the round red and yellow PDO logo, signifying it's the real McCoy.

1. Preheat the oven to 180°C/160°C fan/gas 4. Line a small baking tray with foil.

2. Lightly grease the foil with a smidgen of olive oil, then put the figs, cut-side up, onto the foil and drizzle with the honey and a little swirl of olive oil. Roast for 15 minutes until just soft and the fig juices are beginning to run. Depending on their ripeness, the figs may need 5 minutes longer.

3. Scatter the rocket leaves over a pretty platter. Break up the feta cheese into bite-sized chunks and arrange over the leaves, then nestle in the warm figs. Spoon over the lovely pink syrupy fig juices and season the salad with salt and pepper.

4. In a small ramekin or bowl, loosen the pesto sauce to a dressing consistency with the 1–2 tablespoons of olive oil (depending on the consistency of the pesto) and drizzle this over the salad. Nestle in the Parma ham rolls, scatter with the toasted pine nuts and finish with a generous swirl of olive oil, then serve.

GET AHEAD

• Step 2 can be prepared up to a day in advance. Cool, cover and chill, then bring back to room temperature. Warm through in the oven (temp as above) for a few minutes before assembling the salad and serving. Or serve the figs at room temperature, if you prefer, so no reheating required.

HINTS & TIPS

• For vegetarians, use a feta cheese that is suitable, ensure the pesto sauce is made with a vegetarian Italian-style hard cheese, and omit the Parma ham.

• This also makes a lovely starter for 6–8 people, either served on one platter or on individual plates.

Griddled Pesto Chicken Tenders with Lime Mayo Dip

SERVES 3–4
(or serves more as
part of a picnic)

350g chicken tenders
(inner breast fillets)
4 tablespoons thick mayonnaise
(see notes on page 17)
juice of ½ lime (or more to taste)
2 tablespoons pesto sauce
(see notes on page 17)
1 tablespoon olive oil
salt

GET AHEAD

- Step 1 can be completed up to
2 days in advance. Keep covered
in the fridge.

- Step 2 can be made up to 3 days
in advance. Cover and chill.

- The whole recipe can be completed
up to 2 days in advance, cooled,
covered and chilled. It may lose
some of its vibrant green colour but
will taste exactly the same. Bring
back to room temperature to serve.

HINTS & TIPS

- Don't be tempted to turn the chicken
over if it resists being lifted from the
pan, otherwise the tasty bits will stick
and be left behind on the griddle.

When these are cooking, my children say the smell takes them straight back to school sports day picnics – it's one of their favourites and always requested. The melt-in-the-mouth inner breast fillets are the most tender part of a chicken. Combined with pesto sauce and griddled for a few minutes until lightly charred, these are irresistible, especially when dunked in lime mayo first.

1. Slice the thickest chicken tenders in half horizontally through the middle to produce two flatter, matching pieces. Leave any thinner ones as they are. Aim for all the strips to be roughly the same thickness. Set aside.

2. Mix together the mayonnaise and lime juice in a small bowl, adding more juice to taste if you like, but bearing in mind the consistency for dipping purposes. Set aside.

3. Heat a griddle pan on a high heat until smoking hot. Meanwhile, put the chicken into a mixing bowl with the pesto sauce, olive oil and a generous pinch of salt (or, to save on washing up, mix together in the chicken carton). Combine to coat evenly.

4. Lay the chicken pieces flat on the hot griddle, spacing them out (depending on the size of the griddle pan, you'll need to do this in a few batches, as it's important not to overcrowd the pan, which would reduce the heat and cause the chicken to stew). Cook the chicken for 2–3 minutes until golden brown and a little charred underneath and it willingly lifts from the pan. Leave for a little longer if not, then turn the chicken pieces over to cook for another 2 minutes, until just cooked through. Remove to a serving plate or platter.

5. Serve warm or cold with the lime mayonnaise in a little bowl or pot for dipping.

Desserts in a Dash

Being a bit of a lazy pudding maker, these recipes suit me down to the ground; some are so simple they can barely be described as recipes. How welcome when one's preparing a whole menu, not to have to spend much time on the final course. Almost every recipe can be made in advance – a huge bonus! You'll find a cross-section through the spectrum, from creamy and fruity, to baked and downright indulgent. Great results for minimum effort!

Plum & Almond Cake

110g butter, softened, plus
  extra for greasing
110g self-raising flour
110g caster sugar
½ teaspoon baking powder
2 eggs
100g natural (un-dyed) marzipan,
  cut into small (1cm) dice
8–10 plums (depending on size),
  stoned and quartered
55g amaretti biscuits, roughly
  crushed into varying sizes
  of 'gravel'
1 tablespoon demerara sugar
icing sugar, for dusting
crème fraîche, double cream or
  vanilla ice cream, to serve
  (or try it with the Spiced Plum
  Compote on page 203) (optional)

GET AHEAD

• The cake keeps very well in an
  airtight container or in the fridge
  for 2–3 days. It also freezes
  beautifully (defrost before serving).
  Serve the cake at room temperature
  or reheat in the oven (temp as
  above) for 10–15 minutes until
  warm throughout. I also enjoy
  this particular cake cold straight
  from the fridge.

I usually make this with our Victoria plums in early autumn. There's a surprise in the middle in the form of diced marzipan, adding a wonderful almond flavour. However, I wouldn't mention the 'M' word as it can be controversial! I inadvertently did just that to a dyed-in-the-wool marzipan hater, who had already tried a slice, declared it delicious and could detect no trace of marzipan at all! After all, marzipan is just almonds, and the culprit is usually the manufactured yellow type rather than the pale natural kind. So, don't be put off the recipe for the same reason. The marzipan just distributes a lovely gentle almond flavour throughout the cake.

1. Preheat the oven to 160°C/140°C fan/gas 3. Lightly butter a loose-bottomed, 20cm round cake tin and line the base with a disc of baking parchment.

2. Put the butter, flour, caster sugar, baking powder and eggs into a food-processor and whizz together for 20–25 seconds until well mixed (or, put them into a bowl and beat together by hand or with an electric hand-held mixer to make a soft cake mixture). Spoon the cake mixture into the prepared tin and spread evenly. Scatter with the marzipan and gently press it down into the mixture. Arrange the plums on top, laid on their sides and pushed slightly into the cake mixture. Scatter all but 1 tablespoon of the crushed amaretti evenly over the top, then sprinkle over the demerara sugar.

3. Bake for 1 hour 5 minutes–1¼ hours or until a skewer inserted in the middle comes out clean. If the cake's not quite ready, bake it for a little longer. Remove the cake from the oven, leave it to cool in the tin for 5–10 minutes, then remove it from the tin (keeping it plum-side up) and transfer to a wire rack.

4. The cake can be served warm or at room temperature. Just before serving, scatter with the reserved amaretti crumble and dust the top with icing sugar. Serve with any of the serving suggestions above, if you like.

Spiced Plum Compote

SERVES 4
(or serves 6–8 as an
accompaniment or
for breakfast)

500g plums, halved and stoned
100g caster sugar (more to taste,
  if needed)
2 star anise

GET AHEAD

• The compote will keep for up to
  3 days (or a few more), covered,
  in the fridge. It also freezes
  beautifully – defrost before serving
  cold or reheat gently to serve.

HINTS & TIPS

• The compote is very versatile: enjoy
  it with yoghurt and granola or
  porridge for breakfast; with coconut
  yoghurt (vegan), cream, crème
  fraîche or ice cream as a pudding;
  puréed as the base for a plum fool.

I usually make this luscious, thick compote with our Victoria plums,
which are plentiful in early autumn. Our harvest depends on whether
or not I win the race between the wasps and squirrels, so for this reason,
I aim to pick them when underripe and finish them off in the kitchen.
That said, this recipe works well whether the plums are ripe or not.
A dollop is very good with the Plum and Almond Cake (see page 200).

1. Put all the ingredients into a small saucepan with 1 tablespoon of water
and stir, then simmer on a gentle heat for around 8 minutes, stirring very
gently once or twice. The exact simmering time will depend on the ripeness
of the plums, un-ripe ones taking a bit longer. I aim for a compote which is
soft but still a little chunky when eating as is. However, should you wish to
purée the plums, cook further until soft throughout.

2. Taste and add a little more sugar, if necessary. The syrup will thicken
considerably as it cools. Serve warm, at room temperature or chilled.

Raspberry & White Chocolate Cake

SERVES 6

110g butter, softened,
  plus extra for greasing
110g self-raising flour
110g caster sugar
½ teaspoon baking powder
2 eggs
100g best-quality white
  chocolate, roughly chopped
  into varying sizes of 'gravel'
150g fresh raspberries
icing sugar, for dusting
freeze-dried raspberry powder
  or freeze-dried raspberry pieces,
  to decorate
crème fraîche, double cream,
  thick Greek-style yoghurt
  or vanilla ice cream,
  to serve (optional)

GET AHEAD

• The cake keeps very well in an airtight
container or in the fridge for up to
3 days (or a few more), and can also
be frozen (defrost before eating/
reheating). Serve the cake at room
temperature or warm through in the
oven (temp as above) for around
10 minutes until just warm throughout.

HINTS & TIPS

• Should the cake be slightly soggy
in the very middle when cut into,
this is a joy rather than a mistake!

• I also enjoy this cake cold straight
from the fridge, as flecks of white
chocolate which have permeated
throughout, are set hard.

Raspberries and white chocolate are right up there as far as flavours matched in heaven go! Although rustic, this is quite an indulgent, versatile cake, good as a pudding or for any time of the day. Light and fluffy the day it's cooked, the longer it keeps, the more damp it gets, in a nice syrupy way. So, if you're after a little more moisture, especially if serving as a pudding, make it a day or two in advance.

1. Preheat the oven to 160°C/140°C fan/gas 3. Lightly butter a loose-bottomed, 20cm round cake tin and line the base with a disc of baking parchment.

2. Put the butter, flour, caster sugar, baking powder and eggs into a food-processor and whizz together for 20–25 seconds until well mixed (or, put them into a bowl and beat together by hand or with an electric hand-held mixer to make a soft cake mixture). If using a processor, spoon the cake mixture into the prepared tin and roughly spread out to the sides of the tin. Pile the chopped chocolate and the raspberries into the middle and gently stir to incorporate them into the mixture, avoid disturbing the mixture around the very edges of the tin as best you can, then level out with the back of the spoon. If making in a bowl, very gently fold the chocolate and raspberries into the mixture, then spoon into the tin and spread level.

3. Bake for 55 minutes–1 hour 10 minutes or until a skewer inserted in the middle comes out clean, the cake is shrinking away from the sides of the tin and the top is springy to touch. If it's not quite ready, bake it for a little longer. The length of time varies and will depend on the juiciness of the raspberries. Remove from the oven and leave to cool in the tin for 5–10 minutes, then remove from the tin and transfer to a wire rack. Serve warm or cold.

4. Just before serving, dust the top with icing sugar, then decorate with a dusting of freeze-dried raspberry powder or raspberry pieces, and serve with any of the above suggestions, if you like.

• Blackberries are a lovely substitute
for raspberries. Generally being less
juicy than raspberries, the cake will
only take around 55 minutes to cook.

• Choose best-quality white chocolate
that contains cocoa butter rather
than vegetable oil.

Apricot & Marsala Syllabub

SERVES 4–5

5 tablespoons (75ml) Marsala
2 heaped tablespoons, plus
   2 teaspoons, best-quality
   apricot conserve
300ml double cream, straight
   from the fridge

Possibly the quickest recipe in the book! A lovely, elegant pudding for entertaining, especially when served in pretty glasses. Bear in mind that it's quite alcoholic when it comes to children. This is best made the day before.

1 Put the Marsala, the 2 heaped tablespoons of apricot conserve and the double cream into a blender (not a food processor) and blend briefly together, just until the cream has thickened. Be careful not to over-blend. Alternatively, whisk the ingredients together in a small mixing bowl using an electric hand-held whisk.

2. Spoon into pretty glasses, dishes or small coffee cups, cover and chill for a minimum of 4 hours, but preferably overnight.

3. Put the 2 teaspoons of apricot conserve into a ramekin and stir vigorously with a teaspoon to loosen it. If necessary, add a few drops of hot water to loosen it further. Spoon over the syllabubs to decorate just before serving.

GET AHEAD

• The recipe can be completed up to 3 days in advance, covered and chilled. Decorate as above just before serving.

HINTS & TIPS

• Err on the side of under-whipping the cream as it will thicken up while being spooned into the glasses/ dishes/cups and yet more while it's in the fridge.

• Swap the Marsala for dry sherry or white wine.

Chocolate, Coconut & Ginger Cups

SERVES 4

100g dark chocolate (minimum
   70 per cent cocoa solids)
1 piece of stem ginger in syrup,
   drained and finely chopped, plus
   a little of the syrup for decorating
200g natural coconut yoghurt
   (such as The Coconut Collab)
1 tablespoon icing sugar, sifted

GET AHEAD

• The cups can be made up to
   3 days in advance, covered
   and chilled (although they will
   keep for up to 2 weeks in
   the fridge).

HINTS & TIPS

• The stem ginger (and ginger syrup)
   can be omitted, if you prefer.

• A little finely grated orange zest
   is a nice addition, but omit the
   ginger (and ginger syrup).

Can there be an easier or quicker pudding?! These little chocolate cups are made with natural coconut yoghurt, which, made solely from coconuts, is plant-based, therefore dairy-free, and creates the foundation for a lovely pudding. Although quite rich, the cups aren't at all gloopy or too sweet; indeed, they have an appealing tart, slightly sour tang.

1. Break the chocolate into small pieces and put into a small, heatproof mixing bowl with the chopped stem ginger, reserving ½ teaspoon of the ginger for decoration.

2. Heat the yoghurt and icing sugar together in a small saucepan on a low heat, stirring gently until smooth and just below boiling point. It shouldn't bubble up. Pour this over the chocolate (to cover it) and leave to stand for 3 minutes before very gently folding the yoghurt, chocolate and ginger together, just until it's combined, dark, smooth and glossy. Remember the tiny lumps will be from the ginger, rather than un-melted chocolate, so be careful not to over-mix or stir more than you need to.

3. Spoon into small cups, glasses or ramekins, cool, cover and chill for a minimum of 4 hours, although overnight is best. Decorate with the reserved ginger and a little trickle of its syrup from the jar, before serving.

Baked Apple Granola Crunch

SERVES 5–6

750g cooking apples,
   peeled, quartered, cored
   and thinly sliced
30g caster sugar
½ teaspoon ground cinnamon
250g best-quality granola

This is the speediest apple crumble, which will be as good as the quality of the granola you choose. I like to use a nutty, oaty one that has a few largish clusters throughout, and the odd bit of dried fruit running through it as well. Arguably healthier than traditional crumble, the topping becomes deliciously chewy as it bakes.

1. Preheat the oven to 200°C/180°C fan/gas 6.

2. Put the apples into a shallow, ovenproof dish (I use a 22 x 5cm pie dish) with the sugar and cinnamon and mix together. Level the apples and spoon the granola over the top. Lay a piece of foil loosely over the dish.

3. Bake for 45 minutes, then remove the foil and bake for a further 3–5 minutes or until the top is light golden brown. Leave to cool down before serving lukewarm, although it is also good served cold.

GET AHEAD

- The recipe can be made up to a day in advance (keep loosely covered at room temperature) and warmed through in the oven (temp as above) for 10–15 minutes, loosely covered with foil. Remove the foil for the last few minutes to crisp up, if necessary.

- Keep any leftovers covered in the fridge for up to 3 days (or a little longer). Bring back to room temperature or warm through (as above) before serving.

HINTS & TIPS

- Depending on how sweet your chosen granola is, you may like to add a tablespoon or so more sugar to the apples.

- Make in individual ovenproof dishes, which will take less time to cook, if you like.

- Add some blackberries to the apples, or swap the apples for rhubarb, plums, pears, raspberries, and so on (adjust the quantity of sugar accordingly). The cooking time will be a little shorter.

Lime Posset

SERVES 8

3 limes
600ml double cream
100g caster sugar
diced ripe mango, fresh berries
   and/or small edible flowers,
   such as violas or borage, to
   decorate (optional)

GET AHEAD

• Complete to the end of step 3 up
to 2 days ahead and keep in the
fridge.

HINTS & TIPS

• It's best not to heat cream (or milk
for that matter) in a non-stick pan
as this causes it to form a brown
scorched skin on the bottom of
the pan.

• Add another 50g of sugar if
you prefer a sweeter version.

This is the easiest of puddings and it's always popular. This version, although adequately sweet, is on the tart side, allowing the zing of the lime to sing through. A refreshing, creamy, silky-smooth delight!

1. Grate the zest from two limes, cover and set aside. Squeeze the juice from all three limes.

2. Put the cream and sugar into a pan (not non-stick) large enough for the cream to expand while boiling. On a gentle heat and stirring occasionally to help dissolve the sugar, heat the mixture until it comes to the boil, then boil rapidly for 3 minutes.

3. Remove from the heat, whisk in the lime juice and pour into eight small, heatproof glasses, glass pots, pretty china dishes or tea or coffee cups. Cool, then cover and chill for at least 4 hours until set, although overnight is best.

4. Decorate the top with the reserved lime zest and a little diced mango, some berries and/or edible flowers (if using). Serve.

Blood Orange & Rhubarb Meringue Nests

SERVES 6

2 blood oranges
½ quantity rhubarb from
   the Rhubarb, Elderflower
   & Greek Yoghurt recipe
   (see page 220), cooled
6 ready-made meringue nests
6 heaped tablespoons crème
   fraîche or lightly whipped
   double cream

GET AHEAD

• The rhubarb can be prepared up to
3 days ahead, covered and chilled,
as can the blood oranges and zest.
Chill them individually, then bring
back to room temperature to serve.
The nests can be filled with crème
fraîche or cream an hour or two in
advance and kept somewhere cool,
but leave spooning over the fruit till
just before serving.

HINTS & TIPS

• The No-churn Raspberry Ripple &
Amaretti Ice Cream (see page 223),
tumbled with fresh raspberries
and perhaps some freeze-dried
raspberry pieces and/or powder,
is an alternative filling, as is the
Spiced Plum Compote (see page
203), spooned over the crème
fraîche or cream in the nests.

Since the aim of these recipes is speed, I thought it acceptable to include shop-bought meringue nests in the mix. You may prefer to make your own, but ready-made nests are a great store cupboard standby for a quick pudding (some are better than others, so choose carefully). All that's required is cream of some sort and any variety of seasonal fruit and you're good to go. Please see the *Hints & Tips* for other filling suggestions.

1. Grate the zest from one of the oranges and set aside on a small plate. Peel a few strips of the zest (without any pith) from the second orange, cut into fine shreds and set aside. Peel the oranges with a knife and cut between the membranes into segments – do this over a bowl to collect the juices. Mix with the rhubarb.

2. Arrange the meringue nests on one platter or on individual plates, spoon a tablespoon of crème fraîche or whipped cream into each one, then spoon the fruit mixture over the top with a little of its juice (any leftover juice can be served separately in a small jug). Decorate with the reserved orange zest, and serve.

Baked Frangipane Peaches

SERVES 8

100g butter, softened,
  plus extra for greasing
100g caster sugar
100g ground almonds
1 heaped tablespoon plain flour
1 egg
8 ripe peaches or nectarines,
  halved and stoned
1½–2 tablespoons flaked almonds
icing sugar, for dusting
double cream, crème fraîche
  or scoops of vanilla ice cream,
  to serve (optional)

I've had this idea for filling the cavities of halved, stoned peaches with frangipane for some time, and now it's become a (rather tasty!) reality… a lovely rustic, Sunday lunch-type recipe.

1. Preheat the oven to 200°C/180°C fan/gas 6. Butter a shallow, ovenproof dish large enough to take the halved fruit in one layer, snugly but not tightly packed.

2. Make the frangipane. In a food-processor or bowl, mix together the butter, caster sugar, ground almonds, flour and egg until combined. Place the peach or nectarine halves, cut-side up, in the prepared dish. Divide the frangipane mixture between the fruit halves, piling it up in the middle, then scatter a few flaked almonds over the top of each one.

3. Bake for 25–30 minutes or until the topping is golden brown (if it's getting too brown, cover loosely with foil for the last 5 minutes). Some of the topping will have slid overboard and wrapped itself around the peaches/ nectarines during cooking, which is fine, and delicious all the same!

4. Serve warm (not hot) dusted with icing sugar, and with any of the serving suggestions, if you like.

GET AHEAD

• The frangipane mixture (in step 2) can be made up to 3 days in advance, covered and chilled (although it will last for up to a week). Bring back to room temperature before use. It can also be frozen (defrost before use). The remainder of step 2 (filling fruit halves) can be completed any time on the day and kept at a cool room temperature.

• The whole recipe can be completed up to 2 days in advance. Cool in the dish it's made in, cover and chill, then bring back to room temperature and reheat in the oven (temp as above) for 5–10 minutes until just warm, before serving.

HINTS & TIPS

• To halve the recipe for 4 people, make the full quantity of frangipane and freeze the remaining half for another time (defrost before use).

Strawberries in Marc

SERVES 4

500g strawberries, hulled
  and quartered lengthways
  if large (small ones halved)
1 heaped tablespoon granulated
  sugar (possibly more to taste)
4 tablespoons marc (of your choice),
  or brandy (of your choice)

Marc is a spirit distilled from the leftover pressings of the wine-making process, and it's normally matured in oak wine casks. A unique style of brandy, it has a wonderful distinct oaky flavour. The best-known wine-producing regions of France for marc are Burgundy (Marc de Bourgogne) and Champagne.

Depending on the sweetness of the strawberries, this recipe isn't an exact science, more of a free-form recipe, therefore it involves a bit of trial and error as to how much sugar to add. Use brandy, if you prefer. Be warned, it's very alcoholic!

1. Put the strawberries into a pretty serving dish, such as a glass bowl.

2. Sprinkle over the sugar, followed by the marc or brandy. Mix together very gently, bearing in mind that a metal spoon and too much stirring will bruise the strawberries. I jiggle around the bowl using the back of a wooden spoon. Cover and chill for a minimum of 4 hours, but better still, overnight, giving the strawberries the odd jiggle from time to time. Serve chilled.

GET AHEAD

- The recipe can be completed the day before and kept chilled. Any leftovers will last beyond that (up to 3 days or a little longer), as the strawberries will be preserved in the alcohol.

HINTS & TIPS

- If serving the strawberries as an accompaniment to something else, the recipe will stretch to feed more people.

- Any leftover marc syrup is very good in the bottom of a glass of something fizzy.

- Serving suggestions: light as air, cloud-like, lightly whipped cream is a lovely accompaniment, as is ice cream (vanilla, strawberry or chocolate) or crème fraîche. The strawberries make a lovely accompaniment to many other puddings, such as panna cotta, cheesecakes, meringues, almond cake and to most things chocolatey. Try them with the meringue nests (see page 215).

Rhubarb, Elderflower & Greek Yoghurt with Oat Crunch

SERVES 4

450g rhubarb (ideally young
  pink forced rhubarb)
3 tablespoons caster sugar
3 tablespoons elderflower cordial
  (undiluted), or water
400g thick Greek-style yoghurt
icing sugar, to taste

For the oat crunch
knob of butter (around 15g)
2 tablespoons porridge oats
1 tablespoon demerara sugar

GET AHEAD

• Complete to the end of step 3 up
  to 3 days in advance, cool, cover
  and chill. Complete to the end of
  step 4 up to 3 days in advance
  (keep chilled).

• Step 5 can be completed up to
  3 days in advance, cooled and
  stored in an airtight container at
  room temperature.

HINTS & TIPS

• Dried Rhubarb Ribbons are a pretty
  way to decorate rhubarb puddings.
  Using a vegetable peeler, peel long,
  thin strips off the length of a young
  (pink) rhubarb stem(s). Place on
  a baking sheet lined with baking
  parchment or silicone paper, in a
  single layer, then dry out in a low
  oven (120°C/100°C fan/gas ½)

Layered up in glasses, this looks so pretty, particularly when using tender young pink stems of forced rhubarb and, if you have the inclination, when topped with the optional dried rhubarb ribbons (see *Hints & Tips*). A piece of stem ginger finely chopped, plus a little of its syrup, is a lovely addition to the rhubarb. This recipe works well with almost any fruit compote.

1. Preheat the oven to 200°C/180°C fan/gas 6.

2. Reserve a stem or two of rhubarb if making dried rhubarb ribbons (see *Hints & Tips*). Cut the remainder into chunks about 2.5cm long and spread over the bottom of an ovenproof dish big enough to take the rhubarb roughly in one layer. Sprinkle over the caster sugar and elderflower cordial or water.

3. Bake for 10–12 minutes or until the rhubarb is just tender, yet still holding its shape. The time will depend on the thickness of the rhubarb. Leave to cool in the dish.

4. Set aside 12 nice pieces of rhubarb, for decoration. Using half the remaining rhubarb, spoon it into the bottom of four pretty glasses with a little of its syrup. Mix the yoghurt with some icing sugar to taste (it should be sweetened, but not too sweet) and spoon half of this into the glasses on top of the rhubarb. Repeat the layers with the last of the rhubarb and yoghurt, and then finally arrange the reserved rhubarb pieces on top. Cover and chill well (for several hours, preferably overnight) before serving.

5. For the oat crunch, melt the butter in a small saucepan on a medium-high heat, add the oats and sugar and cook, stirring, for a few minutes until golden brown, caramelised and crunchy. It will firm up more as it cools. Spread out on a plate to cool (it'll be lumpy in places, which is fine).

6. Just before serving very cold straight from the fridge, top each glass with a little oat crunch and decorate with a tangle of dried rhubarb ribbons (if using).

for 20 minutes or so, until completely dried out (drying time will depend on the thickness of the ribbons). Leave to cool, then store in an airtight container – they will keep for several weeks.

• Although this dessert is simplicity itself to make, simplify it further by serving the rhubarb straight from its baking dish with separate bowls of the sweetened Greek yoghurt and the oat crunch alongside.

No-churn Raspberry Ripple & Amaretti Ice Cream

SERVES 10
(makes around 30 scoops/balls)

150g raspberries
600ml double cream
1 x 397g tin sweetened
  condensed milk
1 tablespoon Amaretto
50g amaretti biscuits

GET AHEAD

- Make the ice cream up to 2 months in advance and store as above.

- When entertaining, to make life easier, I pre-scoop balls of ice cream, pile them up in a pretty bowl and re-freeze, ready to serve straight from the freezer when required.

HINTS & TIPS

- If you would rather serve the ice cream in slices, make it in a 24 x 14 x 7cm loaf tin, the same volume as above.

- Serve the ice cream with a few fresh raspberries tumbled over the top, if you like, or use it to replace the cream and fruit filling in the meringue nests (see page 215) and top with raspberries, other berries or sliced ripe peaches.

- If using a metal sieve, don't use a metal spoon when sieving, otherwise the purée will develop a metallic taste.

There's nothing like home-made ice cream for a get-ahead pudding! This no-churn version is a gift any time, but particularly if you don't have an ice-cream machine. It really couldn't be simpler or quicker to make, and the addition of a liqueur prevents it from setting too hard, therefore it's scoop-able (or sliceable) and ready to eat straight from the freezer. A very popular recipe, which is particularly pleasing as it's so easy!

1. Find a deep 1.5 litre (volume) freezerproof container, preferably with a lid. I recommend filling a container with 1.5 litres of water first, to check it's the right size. The ice cream needs some depth if scooping into balls. Or if you prefer, a lined loaf tin is handy for this (see *Hints & Tips*).

2. Put the raspberries into a sieve over a bowl and mash them up with a spoon. Push all the flesh through the sieve with the back of the spoon, until only seeds are left in the sieve. Discard the seeds.

3. Whisk the cream, condensed milk and Amaretto together in a bowl using an electric hand-held whisk or a stand mixer, until it's just holding its shape in soft peaks, being careful not to over-whisk.

4. Crumble the amaretti biscuits into the cream (I crush them roughly, one by one with my fingers straight into the bowl, producing varying-sized pieces of 'rubble') and fold them in.

5. Spoon a third of the cream mixture into the container, then randomly drizzle over a third of the raspberry purée. Repeat this twice with the remaining two-thirds of both mixtures, finishing with raspberry purée drizzled on top. Swirl a round-bladed knife through the cream mixture to create a ripple effect, being careful not to overdo it and lose the effect (see page 198). Place baking parchment, clingfilm or freezer tissue directly on the surface of the ice cream (to exclude any air and prevent crystals forming), put the lid on or cover tightly with clingfilm, and freeze overnight. Scoop into balls, pile into a pretty bowl and serve.

- We often have a glut of raspberries, so I purée and freeze some, making this recipe even quicker. You need about 100g of defrosted purée for this recipe.

Caramelised Pineapple with Yoghurt, Pistachios, Lime & Mint

1kg ready-prepared fresh
  pineapple chunks, drained
4 tablespoons clear honey
750g strained Greek yoghurt
50g (shelled) whole pistachio
  nuts, toasted and chunkily
  chopped (see *Get Ahead*)
2 mint sprigs, leaves picked
  (around 15 largish leaves)
1 lime

GET AHEAD

• Toast (shelled) pistachios in a small,
  dry frying pan on a medium heat
  for a few minutes, stirring, until just
  beginning to brown. Tip onto a plate,
  then chop. The pistachios can be
  toasted as far in advance as you like
  and frozen (defrost before use), or
  toasted up to a week in advance
  and kept in an airtight container.

• Step 1 can be completed up to 3 days
  in advance, cooled, covered and
  chilled. Serve chilled or at room
  temperature.

HINTS & TIPS

• To serve the pineapple warm, return
  it all to the pan and warm through
  on a low heat for a few minutes,
  before spooning it over the yoghurt,
  if you like.

Fresh, light and zingy, this attractive platter is always so popular and creates a lovely ending to dinner or lunch. Happily, once the pineapple is caramelised, it's just a case of assembling the remaining ingredients. Using ready-prepared fresh pineapple speeds things up. It's also best to use strained Greek yoghurt, which is thicker than regular Greek-style yoghurt.

1. Halve any larger pineapple chunks, so they are all roughly the same thickness. Put half the chunks into a large (preferably non-stick) frying pan with 2 tablespoons of honey and cook on a medium-high heat for 8–10 minutes or until golden brown, caramelised and slightly charred underneath. Turn the chunks over with a fish slice and cook for a few minutes longer until the chunks are golden, glossy and shiny all over. Remove to a shallow dish and repeat with the remaining pineapple and honey. Set aside to cool.

2. Spread the yoghurt over a platter, roughly 30cm in diameter. Spoon the pineapple and any juices over the top, leaving a margin of yoghurt showing around the edge, then scatter with the pistachio nuts. Stack the mint leaves up in batches, roll into tight 'cigarettes' and slice very finely into ribbons. Alternatively, use herb scissors for the same effect. Scatter the mint ribbons over the nuts. Grate the zest of the lime directly over the entire dish (reserve the lime to use the juice in another recipe), then serve.

Quick Nibbles & Easy Drinks

Nibbles and canapés should be as small as possible – just one bite. Any bigger and the risk of spilling food down your front is high and is not a good look! Some canapés can be fiddly and time-consuming to make, so those are best left to a professional rather than the home-cook host.

So, with that in mind, all these recipes are simple to make and bite-sized, requiring minimal last-minute primping. They're tasty temptations designed for a small group to enjoy with drinks before dinner.

For the soft drinks, I have concentrated on shrubs, which, as well as being delicious, have many health benefits. They are also flexible as they can be pepped up with some added alcohol, if desired.

Cocktails are fun, festive and redolent of occasion – less everyday than wine or gin and tonic. Not all cocktails can be prepared ahead, but here you'll find straightforward un-fiddly cocktails mixed in jugs. Handy 'cheer' to have made up in the fridge before guests arrive.

Remember to allow time for the drinks to chill properly, plus you'll need a good supply of ice … and don't forget that it's always cocktail hour somewhere!

Curried Butter Bean Dip

SERVES 4–6
(or serves more alongside
other canapés)

1 x 400g tin or jar butter beans,
   drained and rinsed
¼ teaspoon salt
4 tablespoons olive oil,
   plus extra for drizzling
1 tablespoon warm water
1½ teaspoons medium
   curry powder
1 tablespoon fresh lemon juice
nigella or onion seeds,
   for scattering
2–4 tablespoons pre-cooked
   crispy fried onions from
   a tub (more if you like)
freshly chopped parsley or
   coriander, smoked sea salt
   flakes, micro leaves, or snipped
   salad cress, to finish (optional)

Its rich and creamy texture makes this an appealing dip, or, anointed
with some warm charred roasted vegetables or roasted cherry tomatoes,
it makes a lovely small plate as part of a meze. A handy store cupboard
recipe that I like to serve with artisan-style grissini sticks for dipping.
Suitable for vegetarians and vegans.

1. Put the butter beans into a small food-processor bowl with the salt,
3 tablespoons of olive oil and the warm water.

2. Put the last tablespoon of olive oil and the curry powder in a small
saucepan and stir on a medium heat for a few seconds, just until beginning
to sizzle. Pour this over the butter beans. Process the ingredients in step 1
together until smooth, about 3 minutes, scraping the mixture down from
the sides of the bowl every so often with a spatula, then whizz in the lemon
juice. Check the seasoning – it will probably need more salt – and add a
little extra warm water if you prefer a looser consistency.

3. Spread the dip over a pretty plate and swirl circular channels into the
mixture with the back of a spoon. Scatter with nigella or onion seeds and
the crispy fried onions and finish with a swirl of olive oil. Finish with any
of the suggestions, if you like.

GET AHEAD

• Complete to the end of step 2 up to
  3 days in advance, cover and chill.
  Bring back to room temperature to
  serve. If the dip has firmed up more
  than you'd like, thin it with a little
  warm water before serving.

HINTS & TIPS

• Try switching the butter beans for
  tinned or jarred cannellini beans.

1. SPICY BLOODY MARY
(recipe on page 240)

2. SALTED LEMON ALMONDS

Salted Lemon Almonds

MAKES A MEDIUM
BOWLFUL

225g whole almonds, skin-on
juice of 1 large lemon
1 tablespoon sea salt flakes

GET AHEAD

• The nuts will last in an airtight
  container or jar for several months.

I was shown this recipe in Greece by a delightful and very elderly lady dressed from head to toe in black, cooking at her small family café high up in the hills. These are lovely to rustle up for something quick to accompany drinks, or to make as a gift. They are very moreish! Suitable for vegetarians and vegans.

1. In a small bowl, soak the almonds in the lemon juice for around an hour, giving them the odd stir from time to time.

2. Preheat the oven to 180°C/160°C fan/gas 4. Line a (lipped) baking tray or shallow roasting tin with baking parchment or silicone paper.

3. Spoon the nuts into the tray/tin, leaving the liquid behind. Scatter the salt over the nuts, mix together well and spread the nuts out in one layer, shaking the tray/tin as you go.

4. Bake for 10 minutes, then stir the nuts around, turning them over. Bake for a further 3–4 minutes, until crisp and lightly browned. They can burn very easily and quickly so be attentive! Leave to cool in the tray/tin, then store in an airtight jar or container until required.

Mini Asparagus Croustades

MAKES 24

1 box of x 24 ready-made mini
  croustades (such as Rahms)
12 thin asparagus tips
  (I prefer to buy British
  asparagus when in season)
salt and freshly ground
  black pepper

For the filling
1 teaspoon anchovy essence/sauce
1 heaped tablespoon grated
  Parmesan or Pecorino cheese
  (see tip on page 17)
120ml double cream
2 egg yolks
around 1 tablespoon snipped chives
  or freshly chopped parsley

I developed this recipe for a supper club I was hosting in London and was delighted when it went down a storm, with many requests for the recipe. Since then it's become a much-made and much-loved canapé. The anchovy essence/sauce is more of a seasoning than anything – anchovy doubters would never know, so perhaps better not to mention it! For vegetarians, omit the anchovy essence/sauce (adjust the seasoning accordingly) and swap the Parmesan or Pecorino for a vegetarian Italian-style hard cheese.

1. Preheat the oven to 190°C/170°C fan/gas 5.

2. Put the croustades onto a baking sheet in a single layer.

3. Cook the asparagus tips in a pan of boiling well-salted water for 2–3 minutes, until just tender. Drain, refresh and cool under cold running water. Dry on kitchen paper, cut the actual tips off into 3–4cm-long pieces and halve them lengthways (discard the stems, or see *Hints & Tips*). Set aside.

4. In a small jug, mix all the filling ingredients together with a fork, adding some salt and pepper.

5. Carefully fill the croustades three-quarters full with the custard. Put a halved asparagus tip into each croustade, so it's sticking out above the rim at an angle. Bake for 6 minutes or until just set. Leave to cool down a little before serving warm (the croustades will taste of nothing if served piping hot).

GET AHEAD

- Step 3 can be completed up to 2 days in advance – lay out the dried asparagus tips on a plate, cover with clingfilm and keep in the fridge.

- Step 4 can be prepared up to 3 days in advance, covered and chilled.

HINTS & TIPS

- If time allows (although this takes no time at all!), the leftover asparagus stems can be puréed and seasoned (in advance) and a tiny blob piped/dotted onto each croustade just before serving. Alternatively, add the stems to a salad or some scrambled eggs.

1. NEGRONI (recipe on page 241)

2. PARMESAN, CHIVE & ROSEMARY
   POPCORN (recipe on page 234)

3. MINI ASPARAGUS CROUSTADES

Parmesan, Chive & Rosemary Popcorn

MAKES A GOOD-SIZED
BOWLFUL

3 tablespoons olive oil
50g corn kernels (popcorn maize)
4 tablespoons grated Parmesan
  cheese (see tip on page 17)
2 rosemary sprigs, leaves picked
  and finely chopped
2 tablespoons very finely
  snipped chives
salt

Popcorn is very economical, fun to make (especially for children) and it's ready in a matter of minutes. There's no need to go to the expense of buying a popping machine – a large heavy-based saucepan with a tight-fitting lid is all you need. A bag of home-made savoury popcorn makes a lovely present, too. For vegetarians, swap the Parmesan for a vegetarian Italian-style hard cheese. (See image on page 233).

1. Heat 1 tablespoon of olive oil in a large, heavy-based saucepan that has a tight-fitting lid on a medium-high heat. Add the corn kernels, put the lid on and when it starts popping, give the pan the odd shake over the heat for a minute or so, holding on to the lid tightly! As the popping becomes less frequent, remove the pan from the heat, but don't remove the lid, otherwise you'll end up with popcorn all over the kitchen.

2. Once the popping has stopped, tip the popcorn into a large mixing bowl and remove any un-popped kernels. Immediately, while still hot, sprinkle over the remaining 2 tablespoons of oil, the Parmesan, herbs and a little salt. Stir very well to coat all the corn, gathering and scooping the flavourings up from the bottom of the bowl until they are all coating the corn. Tip into a serving bowl and serve.

GET AHEAD

- The recipe can be made the day before, but will need freshening and crisping up in the oven before serving (it can be served cold subsequently). Spread the popcorn out on a large (lipped) baking tray and bake in a preheated moderate oven (180°C/ 160°C fan/gas 4) for about 5 minutes until crunchy and crisp.

HINTS & TIPS

- The saucepan should not be filled more than a quarter full of corn kernels. In fact, less than a quarter full is by far the best to allow for expansion. If you don't have a large pan, pop the corn kernels in batches.

Salami & Radish Cones

MAKES 40–50

30g butter, softened
½ teaspoon anchovy paste
20–25 radishes (see *Hints
   & Tips*), preferably bunched,
   leaves still intact
20–25 thin slices pre-sliced salami,
   such as Milano, each cut in half
40–50 small rocket leaves,
   if needed (for radishes
   without leaves, use a small
   rocket leaf instead)

Savoury, flavoursome salami with a surprise crunch from the radish within. Butter and radishes are a classic pairing and so a little blob of anchovy butter completes these tasty little canapés. Quick and inexpensive, they only take minutes to make. The salami needs to be thinly sliced for these to work. (See image on page 236).

1. Mix the butter and anchovy paste together in a small bowl.

2. Remove the root tails and large leaves from the radishes, leaving behind the small middle leaves. Cut each radish in half, from top to bottom and if possible so that each half retains a piece of leaf. Cut larger radishes into quarters (see *Hints & Tips*).

3. Holding a half slice of salami in one hand (cut edge to the bottom), put a small blob of anchovy butter in the middle (place a small rocket leaf, stem-end down, on the butter if the radishes have no leaves), then place a half (or quarter) piece of radish, cut-side down, on the butter, leaf end uppermost. Fold the salami over the radish, enclosing it to form a pointed cone, with the cut edge forming the point. Secure with a cocktail stick and put onto a serving plate or board, seam-side down. Repeat with the remaining salami, anchovy butter (rocket, if using) and radishes and serve.

GET AHEAD

• The anchovy butter can be made up to a week in advance, covered and chilled. Soften at room temperature before using.

• The cones can be completed any time on the day, covered and chilled. However, if using rocket leaves, slip/tuck them into the cones just before serving. For easy storage, don't attach the cocktail sticks until serving.

HINTS & TIPS

• If the radishes are large, they will need quartering, so you'll only need 10–13.

• A 200g bag of radishes contains roughly 20 radishes.

• Omit the anchovy paste, if you prefer.

1. PITCHER MARGARITA
   (recipe on page 241)

2. SESAME TUNA BITES WITH
   WASABI MAYONNAISE

3. SALAMI & RADISH CONES
   (recipe on page 235)

Sesame Tuna Bites with Wasabi Mayonnaise

MAKES 20–25 BITES

sesame oil, for smearing
1 x 200g very fresh tuna steak,
  around 2.5cm thick
salt
1–2 tablespoons black sesame
  seeds, spread out on a plate
20–25 micro leaves (optional)

For the wasabi mayonnaise
1 tablespoon thick mayonnaise
  (see notes on page 17)
½ teaspoon wasabi paste

GET AHEAD

• The recipe can be completed the
  day before, omitting the mayonnaise
  topping and micro leaves (if using).
  For easy storage, don't attach the
  cocktail sticks until serving. Cover
  with clingfilm and chill. Add the
  mayo topping and micro leaves
  (if using), then the cocktail sticks,
  just before serving.

• Alternatively, top the tuna with
  the mayo in advance, then to
  avoid it coming into contact
  with the clingfilm, stick a few
  strategically placed cocktail
  sticks into the food, then drape
  the clingfilm over the top and chill.

A quick, unfussy little canapé, which stretches a tuna steak a long way.
If you're short of time, skip the wasabi mayo and serve the tuna with a
soy sauce dip, spiced up with a small pinch of dried chilli flakes. Ensure
the tuna is very fresh.

1. Smear a little sesame oil over the tuna steak (both sides), rub in a little salt
and then press the steak down into the sesame seeds to coat both sides (not
the edges).

2. Heat a small, dry frying pan on a high heat until smoking hot and cook
the tuna for 1 minute on each side. Transfer to a cold plate and leave to cool.

3. Mix the wasabi mayonnaise ingredients together in a small bowl.

4. Carefully cut the tuna into 2cm cubes and arrange on a serving plate or
board, sesame-side up. Spoon or pipe a tiny blob of the wasabi mayonnaise
on top of each tuna bite, followed by a micro leaf (if using). Skewer each
bite with a cocktail stick, and serve.

Wonderful Shrubs!

Shrubs open up and aid the digestive system, therefore are a perfect drink to enjoy before eating. Made with vinegar, they have many health benefits; vinegar balances blood sugar levels and is good for the hair and skin, as well as having other advantages. Shrubs are surprisingly quick and easy to make, they don't really have a discernible taste of vinegar and are wonderfully refreshing.

Enjoy these cordials as a non-alcoholic drink diluted with soda or tonic water, still or sparkling mineral water, or pep them up with equal quantities of gin or vodka and some soda or tonic water.

A tip for using muslin (for any occasion), wet the muslin and squeeze out the excess water before using.

Raspberry & Mint Shrub

MAKES 500ML

225g fresh raspberries
50g mint leaves, roughly chopped
500ml cider vinegar
150g granulated sugar

This is a great way of preserving raspberries (and other summer fruits) and, as well as adding a lovely fresh note to the cordial, mint aids digestion.

1. Put the raspberries, mint and cider vinegar into a saucepan and gently heat together on a low heat. Don't allow it to boil. Decant the mixture into a Kilner-style jar, a container with a lid or a bowl, then leave to cool. When cold, cover and leave it to ferment at a cool room temperature for 7 days.

2. On day 7, strain the shrub through a sieve lined with muslin (or similar), into a small saucepan. Add the sugar and warm on a low heat, stirring occasionally, for a few minutes, just until the sugar has dissolved. Don't allow it to boil. Pour into a sterilised bottle and when cold, close with the lid or a cork. Dilute to taste and enjoy, or store the bottle somewhere cool for up to 2 months (store in the fridge, once opened). It will last considerably longer if stored in the fridge.

Grapefruit & Rosemary Shrub

MAKES 500ML

1 grapefruit (pink or regular), peeled and roughly chopped
10g rosemary sprigs, roughly chopped (I snip them with scissors)
500ml cider vinegar
150g granulated sugar

Pleasingly sharp, tangy and refreshing, as you would expect from citrus fruit, but none the poorer for that!

1. Put the grapefruit, rosemary and cider vinegar into a saucepan and gently heat together on a low heat. Don't allow it to boil. Decant the mixture into a Kilner-style jar, a container with a lid or a bowl, then leave to cool. When cold, cover and leave it to ferment at a cool room temperature for 7 days.

2. On day 7, strain the shrub through a sieve lined with muslin (or similar), into a small saucepan. Add the sugar and warm on a low heat, stirring occasionally, for a few minutes, just until the sugar has dissolved. Don't allow it to boil. Pour into a sterilised bottle and when cold, close with the lid or a cork. Dilute to taste and enjoy, or store the bottle somewhere cool for up to 2 months (store in the fridge, once opened). It will last considerably longer if stored in the fridge.

Spicy Bloody Mary

MAKES A JUGFUL
(around 1 litre; about
6 x 150ml glasses)

1 x 946ml bottle Clamato juice,
  chilled from the fridge
2 teaspoons Worcestershire sauce
1 teaspoon Tabasco sauce
½ teaspoon celery salt
generous grinding of black pepper
lots of large ice cubes
vodka or dry sherry, to taste
celery sticks, to serve (optional)

GET AHEAD

- Step 1 can be made up to 3 days
  in advance, covered and chilled.

HINTS & TIPS

- You might like to include other
  ingredients such as fresh lemon
  or lime juice or horseradish sauce,
  all added to taste.

For years I missed out on Bloody Mary, put off by drinking thick tomato juice – until, that is, I discovered Clamato juice (Clamato Tomato Cocktail is its full name), which is a whole different kettle of fish, if you'll excuse the pun. As the name suggests, Clamato contains some clam juice, but don't be put off, there's no discernible clam or indeed fishy taste at all. Considerably thinner than tomato juice, it's much more drinkable as far as I'm concerned. Find Clamato juice alongside other long-life juices in the ambient section of large supermarkets, or buy online.

Spicy Bloody Mary is my husband John's speciality. Every Sunday lunchtime he makes this, his version, so we've tried to capture his exact quantities here. This produces quite a spicy mixture, which is how we like it, possibly more so, even. However, use the recipe as a guide and tinker with the seasonings until you find your preferred taste.

I advise adding the required amount of alcohol to the individual glasses, rather than the jug, thus catering for those who prefer an alcohol-free Virgin Mary, as well. You'll need lots of ice ... (See image on page 230).

1. Pour the chilled Clamato juice into a glass jug, add the Worcestershire sauce, Tabasco, celery salt and black pepper and stir well to mix together. Taste and adjust the seasonings accordingly, if necessary.

2. Fill 'old-fashioned' (squat) or high-ball (tall) tumblers two-thirds full with large ice cubes, pour over a 'nip' (generous or otherwise) of vodka or dry sherry, then pour over the Clamato mixture, not quite filling the glasses to the top. Serve immediately, with a stick of celery in each glass (if using).

Pitcher Margarita

For one glass per person,
you will need:

50ml tequila
25ml Triple Sec (such as Cointreau)
25ml fresh lime juice (2 limes
   produce around 75ml of juice)
salt, spread out on a plate (optional)
lots of large ice cubes

GET AHEAD

• The Margarita mixture can be
   made up to 3 days in advance,
   covered and chilled.

The easiest recipe in the book, and possibly the most dangerous! I generally find cocktails too fruity and sweet, as well as being a bit of a faff to make. Margaritas are neither and certainly hit the spot for me. Refreshing, vibrant and festive, too, if you put the traditional salt around the rim of the glasses. Margaritas can be mixed in a jug in advance and are easy to scale up, which makes them a great (and glamorous) choice when entertaining. You'll need plenty of ice... (See image on page 236).

1. Mix the required amount of tequila, Triple Sec and lime juice together in a jug, cover and chill for as long as possible, but better still, overnight.

2. When ready to serve, if using salt, rub a little of the Margarita mixture around the rim of the glasses with a (clean!) finger (use 'old-fashioned' tumblers), then dip the glasses into the salt, lightly coating the rims.

3. Fill the glasses with large ice cubes and pour over the Margarita mixture, filling the glasses almost to the top. Serve immediately.

Negroni in a Pitcher

For one glass per person,
you will need:

30ml gin
30ml Campari
30ml Rosso Vermouth
lots of ice cubes
a twist of orange zest

GET AHEAD

• Step 1 can be prepared up to
   3 days in advance, as can the
   twists of orange zest (keep both
   chilled separately).

This well-known Italian cocktail certainly gets the party started! Unlike many cocktails that require shaking over ice, Negronis can be made in a large jug ahead of time, chilled until required and then poured into ice-filled 'old-fashioned' tumblers. This is a lovely drink for the summer months. You'll need a good supply of ice. (See image on page 233).

1. Mix the gin, Campari and vermouth together in a large jug, cover and chill for at least 4 hours.

2. Fill 'old-fashioned' tumblers with ice cubes and pour over the Negroni. Garnish each with a twist of orange zest, then serve.

Index

Conversion Charts

Conversions are approximate and have been rounded up or down. Follow one set of measurements only – do not mix metric and imperial.

WEIGHT CONVERSIONS

METRIC	IMPERIAL
10g	¼oz
15g	½oz
20g	¾oz
25g/30g	1oz
35g	1¼oz
40g	1½oz
50g	1¾oz
55g	2oz
60g	2¼oz
70g	2½oz
75g/80g	2¾oz
85g	3oz
100g	3½oz
110g	3¾oz
115g	4oz
120g	4¼oz
125g	4½oz
140g	5oz
150g	5½oz
160g	5¾oz
170g/175g	6oz
180g	6¼oz
200g	7oz
225g	8oz
250g	9oz
280g/285g	10oz
300g	10½oz
320g	11¼oz
325g	11½oz
340g	11¾oz
350g	12oz
375g	13oz
390g	13½oz
400g	14oz
425g	15oz
450g	1lb
500g	1lb 2oz
600g	1lb 5oz
750g	1lb 10oz
900g	2lb
1kg	2lb 4oz
1.3kg	3lb
1.5kg	3lb 5oz
1.6kg	3lb 8oz
2kg	4lb 8oz
2.7kg	6lb

VOLUME CONVERSIONS (LIQUIDS)

METRIC	IMPERIAL	IMPERIAL/CUPS
5ml	1 teaspoon	
15ml	1 tablespoon	
30ml	1fl oz	2 tablespoons
45ml	3 tablespoons	
50ml	2fl oz	
60ml	4 tablespoons	¼ cup
75ml	2½fl oz	⅓ cup
90ml	6 tablespoons	
100ml	3½fl oz	
120ml/125ml	4fl oz	½ cup
150ml	5fl oz (¼ pint)	⅔ cup
175ml	6fl oz	¾ cup
200ml	7fl oz	
225ml	8fl oz	1 cup
250ml	9fl oz	
300ml	10fl oz (½ pint)	
350ml	12fl oz	1½ cups
400ml	14fl oz	
425ml	15fl oz (¾ pint)	
500ml	18fl oz	2 cups
600ml	20fl oz (1 pint)	
700ml	1¼ pints	
900ml	1½ pints	
1 litre	1¾ pints	4 cups
1.2 litres	2 pints	
1.7 litres	3 pints	

VOLUME CONVERSIONS (DRY INGREDIENTS – AN APPROXIMATE GUIDE)

Flour	125g	1 cup
Sugar	200g	1 cup
Butter	225g	1 cup (2 sticks)
Breadcrumbs (dried)	125g	1 cup
Nuts	125g	1 cup
Seeds	160g	1 cup
Dried fruit	150g	1 cup
Dried pulses (large)	175g	1 cup
Grains & small pulses	200g	1 cup

LENGTH

METRIC	IMPERIAL
5mm/½cm	¼ inch
1cm	½ inch
2cm	¾ inch
2.5cm	1 inch
3cm	1¼ inches
4cm	1½ inches
5cm	2 inches
5.5cm	2¼ inches
6cm	2½ inches
7cm	2¾ inches
7.5cm	3 inches
8cm	3¼ inches
9cm	3½ inches
10cm	4 inches
11cm	4¼ inches
12cm	4½ inches
13cm	5 inches
15cm	6 inches
18cm	7 inches
20cm	8 inches
23cm	9 inches
24cm	9½ inches
25cm	10 inches
26cm	10½ inches
27cm	10¾ inches
28cm	11 inches
30cm	12 inches
31cm	12½ inches
33cm	13 inches
34cm	13½ inches
35cm	14 inches
36cm	14¼ inches
38cm	15 inches
40cm	16 inches
41cm	16¼ inches
43cm	17 inches
44cm	17½ inches
46cm	18 inches

OVEN TEMPERATURES

°C	°C WITH FAN	°F	GAS MARK
110°C	90°C	225°F	¼
120°C	100°C	250°F	½
140°C	120°C	275°F	1
150°C	130°C	300°F	2
160°C	140°C	325°F	3
170°C	150°C	340°F	3½
180°C	160°C	350°F	4
190°C	170°C	375°F	5
200°C	180°C	400°F	6
220°C	200°C	425°F	7
230°C	210°C	450°F	8
240°C	220°C	475°F	9

Acknowledgements

A huge amount of teamwork went into producing *Deliciously Simple*. I do so enjoy being part of a team and especially a stellar one like this. I consider myself extremely lucky to be surrounded by such talent, support, thoughtfulness, consideration, spirit and joyfulness.

My wholehearted thanks to...

...the team at Headline Home and in particular my commissioning editor, Anna Steadman, who is always so enthusiastic and encouraging and has my back at all times (and is almost, if not more, as food obsessed as I am!), Kate Miles, Louise Rothwell for production, Rosie Margesson for publicity, Zoe Giles for marketing, and Margaret Gilbey and Nikki Sinclair for proofreading.

To Nathan Burton, such a boundlessly creative designer, and Anne Sheasby, copy editor supreme. To my wonderful, very special agent, Heather Holden-Brown.

To the great and ever-faithful shoot team – brilliant photographer Tony Briscoe, prop stylist wizard Hannah Wilkinson, my ever-willing and smiling daughter Lucy (food stylist and shoot manager), and Alice Joicey (keeper of the props and the sink, and willing runner for emergency ingredients).

To my very kind friend, Amanda Finley, for her diligent testing of many of the recipes.

To Karen Miller for so smoothly running the office side of my life, not to mention the technical side of the Zoom cookery demos!

And lastly, but most definitely not least, my family. John, Flora, Freddie and Luce, who simply could not support me more, and put up with an awful lot! Thank you, thank you. x

First published in 2023 by Headline Home
an imprint of Headline Publishing Group

1

Cataloguing in Publication Data is available from the British Library

ISBN 978 1 4722 9332 9
eBook ISBN 978 1 4722 9333 6

Commissioning Editor: Anna Steadman
Senior Editor: Kate Miles
Design: Nathan Burton
Photography: Tony Briscoe
Stylist/Home Economists: Jane Lovett and Lucy Lovett
Prop Stylist: Hannah Wilkinson
Copy Editor: Anne Sheasby
Proofreaders: Margaret Gilbey and Nikki Sinclair
Indexer: Ruth Ellis

Colour reproduction by Alta Image
Printed and bound in Italy by L.E.G.O. SpA

Headline's policy is to use papers that are natural, renewable and recyclable products and
made from wood grown in sustainable forests. The logging and manufacturing processes
are expected to conform to the environmental regulations of the country of origin.

HEADLINE PUBLISHING GROUP
An Hachette UK Company
Carmelite House
50 Victoria Embankment
London EC4Y 0DZ

www.headline.co.uk
www.hachette.co.uk